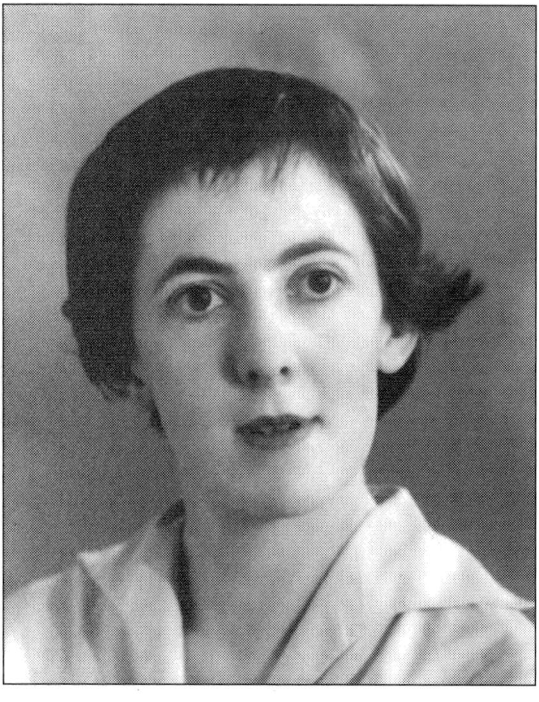

Life Class

THE EDUCATION OF A BIOGRAPHER

Brenda Niall

MELBOURNE
UNIVERSITY
PRESS

MELBOURNE UNIVERSITY PRESS
An imprint of Melbourne University Publishing Limited
187 Grattan Street, Carlton, Victoria 3053, Australia
mup-info@unimelb.edu.au
www.mup.com.au

First published 2007

National Library of Australia Cataloguing-in-Publication entry

Niall, Brenda, 1930–.

Life class: the education of a biographer.

Bibliography.
Includes index.
ISBN 9780522853438 (hbk.).

ISBN 0 522 85343 9 (hbk.).

1. Niall, Brenda, 1930–. 2. Women biographers – Australia – Biography. I. Title

920.72

To my sisters and brothers and
to the memory of our parents,
Francis John Niall 1898–1952 and
Mary Constance Niall 1902–1990.

Contents

Acknowledgements

My warmest thanks to Professor Ian Donaldson for inviting me to give the Inaugural Seymour Lecture in Biography, in Canberra, Perth and Adelaide, in November 2005. Prompted to reflect on my own work, I found that I had more to say than could conveniently be fitted into my lecture, 'Walking Upon Ashes: the Footsteps of a Modern Biographer'. The present book is the result of the overflow of ideas. The lecture, for which Ian Donaldson suggested the title from Dr Johnson, was published by the Humanities Research Centre in Canberra in 2006. It now forms part of Chapter 6 of *Life Class*. As Director of the HRC, and of the recently established Biography Institute, Ian Donaldson has stimulated and helped countless biographical and other scholarly enterprises. Much of my first biography, *Martin Boyd* (1988) was written at the HRC, during two periods as a visiting scholar in the 1980s; and it is a pleasure to acknowledge the friendship and encouragement that began in those years.

Less direct, but also important, are my debts to a number of biographers whose work I admire and whose creative revisitings of their own work have enriched my thinking. These include Richard Holmes' *Footsteps:*

the Adventures of a Romantic Biographer (1983), Michael Holroyd's *Works on Paper: the Craft of Biography and Autobiography* (2002) and Hermione Lee's *Body Parts: Essays on Life Writing* (2005).

In revisiting my published biographies, I am reminded of the generous co-operation of the Boyd family, the McCrae family and Judy Cassab. My work in progress is indebted to the archive of the Jesuit order in Australia, and to the help and interest of its archivist, Michael Head SJ. I thank Peter Walsh and the Eldon Hogan Trust for supporting the Hackett project. Part of Chapter 8 first appeared in Peter Craven (ed.), *Best Australian Essays 2001*.

The early chapters of *Life Class* are drawn mainly from my own memories, but I thank many family members and friends for reminders and corrections. My mistakes, of course, are my own. I am grateful to Helen Elliott, Frances O'Neill and Kate Ryan for reading draft chapters. Rob and Clare Hester solved various research and technological problems. Sybil Nolan, commissioning editor at Melbourne University Publishing, contributed greatly to the shaping of the book, and Wendy Sutherland, as always, has been the editor whose skill every author needs and wants.

Preface

There they are on my bookshelf: four biographies published within a period of nearly twenty years. *Martin Boyd: A Life* (1988); *Georgiana: A Biography of Georgiana McCrae, Painter, Diarist, Pioneer* (1994); *The Boyds: A Family Biography* (2002) and *Judy Cassab: A Portrait* (2005). They don't take up much space on the shelf, but each book represents a bulky archive, a gallery of sights and memories. Filing cabinets overflow with birth, marriage and death certificates, shipping lists and railway timetables, taped interviews, photographs, bibliographies, random jottings of advice to myself. Travel notes from London, Rome, Edinburgh, English villages, castles in Scotland, art galleries in Vienna, Prague and Budapest. Notes from libraries in Melbourne, Sydney, Canberra, London, Cambridge, Edinburgh, Dundee, from a local history collection in Swiss Cottage and a family archive in Chichester.

Some undocumented scenes. Memories of getting lost in country lanes in Gloucestershire, being taken on a 'Martin Boyd walk' in Rome, and searching for Boyd's burial place in Rome's Protestant cemetery, close to the graves of Keats and Shelley. Photographing the Grinling Gibbons font in St James, Piccadilly, where Georgiana

McCrae was baptised in 1804. Standing before the great Brueghel *Peasant Dance* in Vienna's Kunsthistorisches Museum, which the young Hungarian Jewish artist Judy Cassab copied there in 1950. At lunch with Arthur and Yvonne Boyd in the colonial kitchen at Bundanon, their Shoalhaven property. Using a magnifying glass to read the diaries of Arthur Boyd's great-grandmother, with the story of her famous elopement in gold-rush Melbourne in 1855. So much that didn't get into the drafts and print-outs, or the final floppy disks. All these moments, all these people and places, became part of my own life. And although the lives of the dead are complete, untouchable, a biography is, as Richard Holmes has said, 'a handshake across time'.[1]

Not so long ago, biographers were deferential or envious in the presence of novelists. Deferential because the novel is universally acknowledged as an art form, or envious of a novelist's freedom to create. Today it doesn't look so simple. Biographers are well aware that their work has complex possibilities, complex choices. Nearly twenty years after writing my first biography I still meet the same double-edged compliment. 'Reading your book was almost like reading a novel—why don't you try one?' It's still mildly irritating but I no longer feel defensive. This is a golden age of biography. No one who attempts the art practised by Michael Holroyd, Richard Holmes, Hermione Lee, Claire Tomalin, among many others, need apologise for low aim. The standard is dauntingly high. Conscious that they are practising a demanding art, biographers are increasingly aware of novelistic strategies such as structure and point of view. Facts matter; nothing can be done without them; the richer the archive the better the chance of understanding the life it represents. The shaping of that life, and the tone and narrative stance, bring into question the relationship between author and subject. Much of this is mysterious, and perhaps better so. Yet in one way or another, biographers must look inwards as well as outwards. Self-scrutiny for bias or possessiveness, perhaps. 'Whose life is it anyway?' is a question we all should ask.

Self-described as a romantic biographer, Richard Holmes believes that his subjects have always chosen him. At some crucial moment in his life—a crisis in love, or a time of political ferment—a biographical subject has come into focus with a story that must be told. Michael Holroyd, biographer of G.B. Shaw and Augustus John, sees it differently. His career as a biographer, he says, 'probably arose from my need to escape from family involvements and immerse myself in other people's lives'.[2] Yet after those escapes came Holroyd's return to his own story, by way of his eccentric, unhappy family, in *Basil Street Blues*. This was a journey he could not take alone. In his other metaphor for biography, it was a detective story he could not solve on his own.

Every biographer will have a different way of understanding the relationship between self and subject. I think of it as an act of imaginative and creative sympathy rather than romantic identification or possession.

And, rather than an escape, I see biography as a matter of border crossings into other lives, unlike my own, and thereby enlarging understanding, but with a certain degree of connection. As Holmes' metaphor of the handshake suggests, one human being touches and is touched by another. Life stories intersect, however marginally and indirectly. The biographer's relation with the subject may start by being indifferent, even commercial, as just another job, but it won't end that way. Positively or negatively, from idealisation to destructiveness, with finer shades in between, the author's self is always involved.

After four completed biographies and two early attempts, can I see some kind of pattern? Do I respond to stories of displacement, expatriation, exile because these are central to Australian experience? Perhaps so—but not every Australian writes these stories. And having lived almost all my life in the same city, what do I know of exile? Is there something in Erik Erikson's suggestion that the biographer 'projects ... on the men and the times he studies some unlived portions and often the unrealised selves of his own life?'[3] Biography takes time and trouble. What are its processes and rewards? Why were these lives chosen from other possibilities?

Contemplating my own early life, as I've contemplated others, I see an assured place in a privileged family, a good education, for its time, in a period and place almost untouched by war or other external disasters. Not much of a story there. Would anyone want to write this biography? I don't think so. Yet, somewhere in that sedate chronicle there is—or there should be—something to suggest a writer in the making and her biographical impulse. And for all the shelter and safety, there were chilly winds that could not be kept out of the world into which I was born in November 1930, in Melbourne, Australia.

In the closely woven web of memory that makes my own archive, can I disentangle the threads that lead to a late-emerging writer and a happy, though precariously achieved, career as an academic? I didn't expect to become an academic or a biographer. For a woman of my generation it's a surprise to have had any kind of a career, let alone two.

This will not be an autobiography, scarcely even a memoir. Four glimpses of my early life, followed by case studies in which I retrace my own footsteps in the border crossings of four biographies, each one with its own difficulties, its own pleasures and puzzles. And an ending, which marks a new beginning. The hardest part will be to exchange the biographer's third person voice for the first person singular, which I've used sparingly over the years. But at seventy-five, why not?

I

First Lessons

1

On Kew Hill

In 1935, the year before I started school, my parents were building a house. My mother, who in later times might have been an architect or interior designer, visited the site nearly every day to make sure that her ideas were being carried out. Sometimes the architect would be there, and she would have long talks with him, from which I remember nothing except that she called him Mr Jorgensen, while my father called him Ole, a name I had never heard before. Sometimes the garden designer Mr Hammond (Eric) was there, making little drawings and talking about slates and rocks for the terraced garden. The site was on Studley Park Road, a short distance up the hill from Kew Junction, where an old house had been demolished. My parents bought the two blocks that fronted the main road. This gave them the corner site on which to build a north–south tennis court beside the house; and with it came the naming of the little street on which other new houses would soon follow ours. They called it Merrion Place, after Merrion Square in Dublin, whose Georgian symmetry they had admired a few years earlier. Our house, Merrion, was neo-Georgian in style; and one reason for my mother's vigilance was her suspicion that, left to himself, Ole Jorgensen—brother of the more famous Justus who created the operatic extravaganza Montsalvat at Eltham—would add non-Georgian flourishes of his own. Ole Jorgensen, architect of the Xavier College Chapel, liked his work to be visible. My mother's insistence on a high fence disappointed him; and it may have been in protest that he created a little decorative motif in plaster above the front door. O-shaped: was it O for Ole? By the time anyone noticed, it was too late to complain.

There was not much for me to do during my mother's conferences with Mr Jorgensen, except to climb in and out of the half-constructed rooms, wondering which one would be which. Because of the steep slope and the levelling needed to make the tennis court, part of the site was excavated to a depth of five or six feet. Stirring the soft, newly turned soil with a long stick, I found fragments of china, some in richly coloured patterns of flowers and fruit. Here and there the light caught a broken bottle or a fragment of crystal. These belonged to the old house, demolished to make room for ours. I didn't regret the demolition, partly because of the excitement of building something new, but also because of these buried treasures. It was said that the 'old Peacock house', as it was called, had been the scene of a murder. Who was murdered, and by whom, I have no idea, but it produced an agreeable shudder. Reassured that our own house was on the site of the old stables, at a safe distance from any sinister reminders, I set about my excavations in the hope of matching pieces of broken china so as to make a complete plate or at least a saucer. Of course I never did, but there were sufficient numbers of exquisite fragments to keep me hopeful that one day the missing pieces might appear. By the time Mr Hammond's men unloaded their cargo of grey-blue slate, rocks and boulders, to make the terraced garden, I had a small hoard of delicate pieces of bone china from a Victorian dinner service that might have been used by the unhappy Peacock family. That story might serve as a prefiguring of my future career as a biographer, with the lesson, learned early, that there are always missing pieces; you never see the complete design.

Revisiting the Studley Park house in memory I see it room by room, with scenes from childhood enacted in each one. Nearly all the memories are happy, but the one I can't leave out of any account of myself is that of illness and convalescence, reading and being read to, in a sunny upstairs bedroom, with my bed pushed close to the windows that faced north and east, so as to get the best view of Studley Park Road. From the age of three months I had severe asthma attacks which were still quite frequent in the first few years at school. Asthma could be life-threatening, and the only treatment at that time was an adrenalin injection at carefully monitored intervals. Because in those traffic-free days my father could get home from his Collins Street medical practice in fifteen minutes, he was always there when adrenalin was needed. Propped up with four or five pillows, I watched the passers-by from my high window vantage point. 'Make it stop!' I demanded when breathing was painfully constricted. Then, 'Tell me something!' or 'Read me something!' These imperatives delivered stories, some real, some invented or embroidered a bit to make them more diverting. New books were another reward. My father used to drop in at the Hill of Content bookshop in the city, and from there he brought home Ida Rentoul Outhwaite's *The Enchanted Forest.* Later, one by one, he added its three successors, all sumptuously illustrated folio-size volumes, very expensive at five shillings each.

My strongest memory is my mother's anxiety until we heard the sound of the car and my father's quick footsteps on the stairs. Deft and resourceful in everything else, she could never learn to give the injections herself. Her relief, when my breathing eased, was almost inseparable from my own. 'You're better!' she would exclaim, in a tone of such happiness that I felt I'd given her a present, or been given one. And although she told me more than once (did I ask?—I don't remember) that no one ever died from asthma, I wasn't sure she was telling the truth—and of course she was not. The best guarantee, though it carried a freight of unacknowledged fears, was her own story. She had survived childhood asthma in far harder circumstances than mine and had no trace of it in adult life. As a country child in horse and buggy days, she had to wait many hours for a doctor whose only remedy was a dose of castor oil. Her father died when she was five; her English-born mother was lonely and fearful on their country property. My illnesses, which must have revived the terrors of those days, kept me close to both parents, an indulged and protected child, knowing my own importance at home, yet timid outside it, dependent on books and storytelling, used to keeping quiet and staying inside on cold days.

When I was eight I was taken out of school for a year, so as to avoid the respiratory infections that led to bronchitis and asthma. Missing lessons didn't matter, though it left me permanently backward in arithmetic. I had been reading fluently since the age of three. I was ready for the Billabong books and *Anne of Green Gables* at five; and at seven started on Agatha Christie with *The ABC Murders*, chosen because I thought it must be the first of a series. In some families such precocious reading might have made me seem a *wunderkind.* Luckily for me, my older sister and brother, Philippa and John, also read early, fast and often. The third of six children, I remained the cossetted youngest until I was nearly seven, old enough to be excited and proprietorial on the birth of a second brother, Hugh, in 1937. Two more sisters,

Margaret, born in 1939, and Frances, in 1946, completed our widely spaced family. To our shared irritation in later years, we were known as 'a clever family'. True enough: all six of us went to Melbourne University and all did postgraduate degrees. Yet the image of six studious heads bent over our books left out a lot.

My year at home as an eight-year-old was a defining one. With an unusually large share of my mother's company I had an education in family history and storytelling. As we made the beds every morning I used to ask questions about her country childhood. Having read all Mary Grant Bruce's Billabong books, I was fascinated with the thought that my mother had ridden her pony to collect the mail at a little township in New South Wales, had helped to round up sheep, gone out rabbit-shooting at dusk with her brothers, been sent, unwillingly, to boarding school in Melbourne—just like Norah Linton. 'We weren't rich, like the Lintons', my mother would insist, bringing me down to earth. All the same, it sounded wonderful, and I could hear the note of longing in her voice as she described it all. As well as the stories of her country childhood, she talked about the people she remembered: the uncles and aunts and cousins of an extended family whose properties in the Riverina were within easy visiting distance of one another. Although I never saw this fabled territory, it became as complete in my imagination as Faulkner's Yoknapatawpha County was to its creator. I knew its private histories; I could have drawn its map. And because my mother had an analytical, non-judgemental habit of mind, she was easily led into musings about odd behaviour, or even bad behaviour. 'I don't know why he—or she—turned out like that', she would say, before giving her own idea of just what might have gone wrong with an errant cousin.

Most of her stories fitted the facts as I later knew them; and her observations of character were acute and perceptive. But now and then I learned a lesson in the unreliability of memory. I liked the tale of Aunt Mary, who built herself a tree house to which she would retreat to write short devotional fiction for the *Messenger of the Sacred Heart*, a Melbourne Catholic monthly. When a story was completed, addressed and stamped, Aunt Mary would drop it down from her eyrie, calling for one of her sons to saddle his pony and ride three miles to post it for her. This beguiling anecdote was flatly contradicted, years later, by one of my mother's brothers, whose version of the past was less interesting but more likely. 'A tree house? Nonsense. She had a cabin in the garden. And I don't know why you think she was some kind of a bush carpenter. Aunt Mary wouldn't have known which end of a hammer was which.'

Several strands in the family story took on special importance in my year out of school. It was 1939, and the outbreak of the Second World War in September of that year had my mother musing on 1914, when she was twelve years old. With two sons of military age, her family was shaken by the choices and the temper of the time. A dictatorial uncle, guardian of this fatherless family, told the eldest son, my uncle Jack, that it was his duty to volunteer. Jack was just then preparing for medical school. His instincts and all his reading at that time had turned him towards pacifism. My English-born grandmother, angry at so much pressure on her son, put it down to the Irish-Australian family's fear of being stigmatised as anti-British in a rural community where patriotic feeling was running high. She wrote frantic letters to one of her brothers in England; somehow strings were pulled and, instead of joining the AIF, Jack sailed to London as a civilian, where by some strategy I don't understand he joined the Canadian Expeditionary Force. He then spent the war years as a medical orderly, tending the wounded and dying as they were shipped back from the trenches—a searing experience that confirmed his pacifist instincts as well as his choice of a career in medicine.

This wartime story brought my grandmother into the narrative. Knowing her then as a benign old lady who collapsed in helpless laughter while reading us the *Just So Stories*, I had to adjust my vision to take in the distraught mother of 1914. Widowed young, she brought up her seven children on her husband's property, but was never at home in Australian bush life. A competent manager of her household, she never learned to ride and it was said that she could distinguish only one of their horses, because it was grey. As soon as her second son was ready to manage the property, she retired to Melbourne with her two daughters and two medical student sons. Her nostalgia was all for England, to which she returned for two long visits, and like all her generation she invariably spoke of it as 'home'.

These two stories from the family narrative came to mind many years later. Writing about Martin Boyd, an unwilling participant in the First World War, took on an added resonance because my uncle's wartime ordeal had so impressed my eight-year-old self. And although I didn't realise it at the time of writing, I think that images of my grandmother, lonely and displaced in the Australian bush, contributed to my understanding of Georgiana McCrae, whose story, in my second biography, is one of exile.

My father's legacy to a future biographer is less apparent than that of my mother, who was the primary storyteller. Yet I can see now that his physician's gifts for observation, empathy and intuition were central lessons. With or without a stethoscope he was a good listener. Medical students and young residents at St Vincent's Hospital remembered his ward rounds for the persistence with which he pursued a case history. He didn't go in for brilliant guesses. If it seemed that something was missing in a diagnosis the examination had to be done all over again. He was not one of the hospital's autocrats, but he insisted on courtesy to the public patients, who must be called by their names; Mr, not Bill or Joe, and Miss or Mrs, never 'dear'. When the annual Melbourne University exams in medicine came round, his study floor was laid out like a card table with the good, the bad and the indifferent in graded groups of student scripts.

These drew sighs and groans at the handwriting and prose style of many, but huge pleasure at talent which the exams revealed or confirmed. I didn't see my father with his patients, but while doing my homework, half-listening to his evening phone calls to GPs, I used to wonder how to spell interesting new words like myocardial infarct or pneumothorax. Later I had some sense of the human element in each report, and the intellectual energy that went into his work. The phone calls done, he would settle down to his medical journals, not as a chore but in search of ideas. His bedside book for several years was Boswell's *Life of Dr Johnson*, because it closed off the day's problems, and it didn't matter if he never finished it.

My parents would often take a walk after dinner ('just to Burke Hall and back') to talk over the day's happenings. Yet they had their almost self-contained spheres: his work, her household. His views were often refracted through her, or presented as 'we think'; and it was only on holidays that we got the full share of his attention, at least in the war years. At that time, with many of his colleagues away on military service, his clinical teaching and examining commitments were doubled, and his private practice must also have increased. Our house ran to timetable so that he could get through the evening's work. He did hospital visits on Saturday and Sunday mornings and, apart from Saturday afternoon tennis and Sunday dinner at our Niall grandmother's house, he seldom took time off. My mother's time was less structured. She ran her household smoothly, with no apparent effort, and was happiest when she had a project to take her outside it. In a period when many wives had to ask for money or at least account for their spending, she had her own cheque book and did as she pleased with the family income—within reason, as she would have said, but with some exhilarating moments when her imagination took over.

On one such impulse, on Cup Day 1940, more than a year after the declaration of the Second World War, she and my father took a drive into the country, just to look at a little farm she had seen advertised, at Tallarook, near Seymour, less than two hours' drive from Melbourne. 'Just looking' usually meant serious purpose; and sure enough, they bought it on the spot: sixty acres of fertile land with a tumbledown farmhouse on a steep hill. A creek ran through it, tributary of the Goulburn River. Owned by an elderly Scottish couple, the farm was called Bonnie View. Our near neighbour, owner of the large and perfectly maintained property, Landscape, was Essington Lewis, chairman of Broken Hill Proprietary, and newly appointed as Director-General of Munitions. Invited to afternoon tea at Landscape or to go out riding with friendly and accomplished twelve-year-old Jane Lewis, we had an authentic glimpse of the Billabong world of Mary Grant Bruce, but run with even more efficiency. Every tool in every shed was in its numbered place: you could see why Essington Lewis had been given charge of our war effort.

One reason for buying the farm was my mother's love of the land, her nostalgia for her own country childhood.

Another reason, as I later discovered, was to help me outgrow my asthma, and in this it worked brilliantly. I had refused to learn tennis, and was a lacklustre conscript in swimming lessons at the City Baths, but from the first day at the Misses Irving's Waverley Riding School, in semi-pastoral Burwood, I was like every other nine-year-old, in love with the whole world of horses. Elizabeth Taylor in *National Velvet* became my role model. Seeing me so eager to go to my riding lessons every Saturday, by tram and train, with schoolfriends, my parents acted with their usual wholeheartedness. They could have just bought me a pony and kept it at the riding school. A complete farm, long before hobby farms became tax incentives, was a large gesture. It made me an outdoor child, absorbed in riding, interested in the menagerie of dogs and horses, hens and chickens, cows and sheep, which my mother, a natural organiser, assembled in record time. I can't imagine how she managed to get the four-bedroom house renovated, painted, furnished and lit with kerosene lamps, nor how she had the outbuildings and fences repaired, ordered farm machinery, matched a governess cart with a horse broken to harness, chosen safe children's ponies, bought saddles and bridles, and much more besides. Bought in early November, the farm was ready for the Easter holidays. When petrol was rationed, my father fitted a gas producer to his car, for which he burned logs for charcoal in a picturesque ritual beside the creek. We spent many weekends and holidays at the farm throughout the war years, often taking the train so that we could bring schoolfriends with us, and being met by governess cart at the little Tallarook station. We all listened to the bad news from Europe and later from the Pacific that came through on our cumbersome battery-operated wireless, but for me at least the adults' worries were dissipated in the enchantments of Tallarook. I didn't read during those holidays; none of us did. With eight children, age range from two to fourteen, which included three schoolfriends, in a small house, it wasn't quiet. At night we played cards and Consequences under the soft light of a kerosene lamp, and took candles to bed. At home I had stubbornly resisted the breathing exercises prescribed for asthmatics. Here, if I wanted to ride, I had to catch and saddle my pony, which was half an hour's exercise in itself. The steep hill, on which we used to toboggan on a tin tray, was a constant breathing lesson. The idea of swimming, so unattractive at the City Baths, became quite appealing in the creek, in spite of sharp stones on the uneven creek bed and regular encounters with leeches.

The farm went into decline when Simmie, the gentle old man who looked after it for us, unexpectedly married and departed. His hastily chosen successor, who happened to be the local SP bookmaker, brought shady company to Bonnie View—even a police raid on his cottage—and the farm work was neglected. I was by now free of asthma, and at fifteen was outgrowing my passion for horses. Like my classmates, I was collecting pictures of Test cricketers at the time of the first postwar

England tour; and was in love with film star Gregory Peck. My older sister and brother, having left school, had the competing interests of university life. John was living in college, Philippa's social life filled her weekends. The three younger children would probably have enjoyed more time at Tallarook, but they didn't get the chance. We sold the farm and bought a holiday house in Mornington. Closer to home and much less trouble, it pleased everyone, especially my father who loved the sea. At the farm he was never closely engaged, as my mother was. In the evening he trimmed the lamps, brought in wood, made the fire, played cards with us all—but what was he doing all day? I remember him vainly trying to persuade Simmie, a former boundary rider who lived on tinned beef, fruitcake, black tea and beer, to change his diet. He took charge of the incubator that was installed at home in a room behind the garage, and brought in the new-born chicks on a tray to the warmth of our playroom fire. He also diagnosed some ailment among the hens. His clinician self didn't readily take a holiday.

Regretfully, with the sale of the farm, I said goodbye to my pony, for whom a good home was found, and with five guineas from the sale of my saddle and bridle I went into Robertson and Mullens bookshop in the city and spent the lot extravagantly on one purchase from the secondhand department: the beautifully bound, gilt-edged 12-volume Edinburgh edition of the complete works of Jane Austen. After an idyllic pastoral interlude, I was back in the world of books, school and home in the first postwar years. Tallarook had been a wonderful diversion, Mornington became a pleasure. Kew was daily reality.

Since we left it, late in 1951, Studley Park Road has changed a good deal but enough remains to prompt memories of growing up there. As a suburb, Kew had a distinctive quality. It was not like South Yarra, an establishment enclave, nor Toorak where, from the mid-nineteenth century, the socially ambitious rich clustered around the Governor's mansion, Toorak House, which predated today's Government House. The picturesque bend in the Yarra River and the many acres of riverside Crown land gave Kew a quiet semi-rural quality. It had a few big houses, including Sir William Stawell's D'Estaville, and David Syme's Blythswood, but these were not on the grand scale of the Armytages' Como in South Yarra or Robert Simson's Leura in Toorak. As the early Kew property owners sold off land in the 1920s and 1930s, the resulting subdivisions drew business and professional men who wanted to be near the city. Studley Park Hill, high above the river's mists and fogs, was thought healthy: a good place to bring up a family.

For Catholic families like ours it had the special appeal of being close to the Jesuit boys' school Xavier College, established in 1878, and its preparatory school Burke Hall. And not far away, in Cotham Road, was Genazzano Convent, which since 1889 had been advertising the 'high and salubrious situation' in which a French order of nuns offered an education for young ladies, either as day pupils or boarders.

These schools, especially Xavier, created the Catholic Kew that I remember: so many houses from whose gates each morning came boys in grey suits and black-and-red caps bound for Xavier, and girls in Genazzano's navy tunics, navy blazers and uncompromising grey felt hats. On Sundays and holy days we would see one another at the Sacred Heart Church, or for variety and perhaps a better sermon, at the Jesuit Church of the Immaculate Conception in Glenferrie Road, Hawthorn.

The Studley Park boys walked to Xavier; the girls caught the tram, most of them to Genazzano. A few changed trams at Glenferrie Road, for the Loreto Convent, Mandeville Hall, or the Brigidines at Kildara. It was harder to get to Sacre Coeur in Burke Road, Glen Iris, so some Kew girls went there as boarders. There were girls in Ruyton and Methodist Ladies' College uniforms at the Kew Junction tram stop but we did not know them. Trinity Grammar boys snatched Xavier boys' caps, and had theirs snatched in return. Whose territory was it? We were a minority, but a substantial one. The Clifton Hotel (renamed as Kew Hotel) still stands, where once a melancholy Mrs Ryan looked out from an upper window. Above it, after a decade or two of sleazy sexual enticements ('foxy ladies') unimaginable in the 1930s and 1940s, advertisements for Toshiba now beckon the IT generation. The site of Reen's Milk Bar on the corner of Princess Street and Studley Park Road disappeared when Kew Junction was widened. Gone too is Dickson's Pharmacy, on the opposite corner, where the pharmacist was Mr Whittaker, father of the splendidly named trio of boys, Howard, Geoffrey and Lionel, all at Xavier. Pretty, dark-haired Ruth Reen made milk-shakes for Xavier boys and, less often, for Genazzano girls. While we were in uniform, all milk bars were out of bounds, because of the presence of Xavier boys. To meet Scotch College or Trinity Grammar boys would surely have been worse, but I cannot remember that they were ever mentioned. They were outside the pale—or we were outside it, depending on which way you looked at the social and religious divide.

Our house, on the first corner, was directly opposite that of Dr Alfred Derham and his artist wife Frances, parents of the future Melbourne University vice-chancellor Sir David Derham. Beside the Derhams was the tall grey Italianate house of Miss Marie de Bavay, whose nephew Xavier de Bavay, naturally, was at Xavier. My parents exchanged calls with the Derhams, but were more friendly with Miss de Bavay, whom I remember for her shortbread biscuits and her very dark sitting room. For a time the Derham and the de Bavay houses were merged into St Paul's School for the Blind: now only the de Bavays' survives.

On our side of the road the Catholic presence included the solid white stucco 1930s house of Captain Henry Curmi, Commissioner for Malta, his English wife Bessie and their five children. Next to them the Chamberlins, Mick (later Sir Michael, businessman and first deputy chancellor of Monash University) and his wife Vera. Then came Lowan, home of Dr Edward Ryan, whose youngest son Maurice was to marry my sister Philippa. Lowan's previous owner, Count O'Loghlin (who used his Papal title) had named it more grandly as Tara Hall. This evoked Moore's *Irish Melodies*, not the white-pillared Tara for which Scarlett O'Hara fought the Civil War. It was a red-brick 1890s mansion complete with gables and gargoyles and a magnificent curving staircase. Behind the Chamberlins was the old Henty house, Field Place, the town residence of pioneer settler Francis Henty from 1873. Shorn of its frontage to Studley Park Road, except for an unweeded drive, it was still occupied by a Henty great-granddaughter, Miss Ruby Hindson, whom we occasionally glimpsed in her garden with another old lady, perhaps her companion. Field Place had once stretched from Studley Park Road to Stevenson Street, with its eastern boundary close to Kew Junction. When a series of subdivisions opened up the Henty acres, there was a large inviting space for Catholic newcomers within an easy distance of Xavier and Genazzano.

We were the new invaders, the families of doctors, lawyers and businessmen, all marking professional success by building houses in the 1930s. My parents chose Studley Park because it was close to St Vincent's Hospital, where my father was an honorary physician, and to his rooms in Collins Street. During his school years at Xavier his family had lived close by in Wellington Street, so Kew was home ground to him, as it was to a lesser degree to my mother, a boarder at Genazzano during the First World War. These two schools drew a disproportionate number of Catholics to Kew. We were not, of course, the sole possessors of the territory, but today as I walk up Studley Park hill, turning first left at Howard Street, along Stevenson Street and back by way of Tara Avenue and Highfield Grove to our Merrion Place corner, I pass the remembered houses (some demolished, some still standing) of dozens of the children we played with in the 1940s.

Before turning into Stevenson Street, home of our friends the Burnes and the Codys, and of the Carmelite nuns in their high-walled monastery, Howard Street makes me pause. Here, during his time as Leader of the Opposition and his first years as Prime Minister, lived Robert Menzies, at 10 Howard Street. Opposite the Menzies house were three families we knew well: the Parers at Number 13, the Dillons at Number 15 and the Curtains at Number 17. Salvatore Parer sent his two sons to Xavier, as did Joe Dillon and Cyril Curtain who each had three boys. From the late 1930s three garden gates in Howard Street would have opened for eight little boys in Xavier's distinctive black and red caps. The only girl from this trio of Catholic houses was Marie Parer, in her Loreto blue uniform, bound for Mandeville Hall, Toorak. Did she and Heather Menzies, a year or two younger, on her way to school at Ruyton, walk together to the tram stop? I think they sometimes did. Pauline Grutzner, from a Genazzano–Xavier family in Stevenson Street, remembers friendly exchanges with the Menzies children. Peter Burne used to play with the Menzies boys. But it would have been unthinkable for one of the Parer boys, tall and impeccably polite, with Spanish good looks, to have invited Heather Menzies to the Xavier Ball, not because she was the cherished only daughter of the Prime Minister, but because of the Catholic–Protestant divide. The Rector of Xavier would have taken a stern view, as would both sets of parents.

We had only one encounter with Mr Menzies. In a rare example of Studley Park graffiti, someone chose our fence for an anti-Menzies slogan. 'Keep Czar Menzies Out!' it urged in emphatic white paint on the dark brown surface. The lettering was visible to every passing car on this busy road that was also a bus route through Collingwood and Carlton to the city. I don't know whether or not my father voted Liberal. My mother voted Labor, mainly because in that early postwar period she reasoned that in the Kooyong electorate Menzies couldn't lose; and it was bad for him to have too big a majority. At any rate my parents didn't feel strongly enough to take quick action on the graffiti. This brought a sharp rebuke from our neighbour Mr Titmuss: 'If you don't remove those words people will think you're in sympathy with them'. Next came Heather Menzies, who chalked her own comment in large letters underneath: 'HOOEY!' Mr Menzies telephoned before calling in to apologise for his daughter, and eventually someone removed the dialogue.

Living in Howard Street, before he became Prime Minister for the second time in 1949, Menzies had more interesting neighbours than the Nialls. A short distance up the hill in Studley Park Road, almost opposite the Pallotine Missionary Fathers' establishment, was Archbishop Mannix's Raheen, red brick with a tower, set well back from the road, behind a circular drive, shaded by old trees. On the other side, a little further on, was a 1930s house built for Jack Galbally, lawyer and State Labor politician, older brother of the more famous barrister Frank. At the top of the hill, beside Burke Hall, was the imposing white mansion of another Catholic, John Wren, an entrepreneur of some notoriety whose great wealth was founded in the illegal gambling industry. Did Menzies know Mannix, Galbally and Wren? Impossible not to have seen the highly visible Mannix whose daily walk from Raheen to St Patrick's Cathedral, in his frock coat and top hat, was as predictable as the bus timetable.

I can't remember Mrs Menzies (Dame Pattie, as she became) doing the shopping, but because all the tradesmen delivered there was very little reason to enter their shops. She must have dealt by phone at least with Old Xaverian Ted Marsh, owner of the butcher's shop in Kew's High Street, whose daughter Diana was at Genazzano. Murphy's Grocery and Laracy's Newsagency reinforced the Irish–Australian element in High Street. The Menzies house would have been fuelled from the wood yard of the Carrucans, who had two daughters at Genazzano. Presiding at the Kew Post Office was Mrs Alma Capes, a widow with children at Xavier and Genazzano.

If Heather Menzies wanted driving lessons, there was Mrs Leonie Porter, another widow, educated at Genazzano, who gave instructions at the Alice Anderson School of Motoring. The car of choice in Kew, patronised by Archbishop Mannix, Sir Geoffrey Syme of *The Age*, and many other families as the alternative to a humble Yellow Cab, was a Humber from Carr's Motors, chauffeur-driven by Old Xaverian Dick Carr or his mother, who always drove Lady Syme. Did Dame Pattie join the Kipling Lending Library? If so, she would have had her books stamped by Mrs Power, whose daughter, the beautiful Helen Power, educated at Genazzano, worked at the Central Catholic Library in Collins Street where she met her future husband Bob Santamaria. This son of an Italian family in Brunswick would later bring an explosive element into a Catholic community, mainly from an Irish background, which by the late 1930s was forgetting the divisions of the First World War, when Archbishop Mannix was a focus of anti-Catholic bitterness because of his opposition to conscription and his open support of the Irish Republican movement.

Between the wars the religious divide was perhaps best seen as a truce. No one wanted to bring down the fences. Ecumenism was not in anyone's vocabulary. The arrogance with which we divided the world into two blocs—Catholic and non-Catholic—is hard to imagine today. Yet so it was. There was no reason to think about Anglican, Presbyterian or Methodist, with whose Christian beliefs we had so much in common, nor Jews whose traditions we had inherited. Aborigines we never saw; Asian migration was far in the future; Muslims were unthinkably exotic. Our immediate neighbours, unless they shared our beliefs, our churches and schools, were almost invisible. Invisible, not hostile. At least that's my memory of the non-Catholic neighbours on Kew Hill and elsewhere. That there had been hostility I vaguely knew, but because my parents had grown up without meeting discrimination except of a very minor kind, we didn't inherit any sense of threat.

My father, who had been a resident at the Royal Melbourne Hospital in 1920, was said to have been lucky to get a place there because that hospital didn't normally take Catholics. His colleagues at St Vincent's were nearly all Catholics, as were most of the tenants at 33 Collins Street, where he and two of his brothers had ground-floor rooms next to those of our Studley Park neighbour, ophthalmologist Edward Ryan, who owned the building. My father's fellow members of a small research group of cardiologists, however, came from the Alfred and the Royal Melbourne. Once, when it was his turn to be host for the meeting, I was sent in with the tea and sandwiches. No ham sandwiches, I was told, Dr Rothstadt and Dr Kaye are coming. This introduction to Jewish customs seemed a small variation on our own meatless Friday rule, and I can't remember taking any interest, except to register that tall, fair Dr Rothstadt, in a pale grey suit, was the nicest of the visitors because he helped with the teacups while the others went on talking.

Another meeting at our house suggests that my father had friends on both sides of the political divide. Quietly reasonable, he was good at conflict resolution. Two men in dark overcoats, arriving separately one winter night for a secret meeting, were Senator Nick McKenna, Minister for Health in the Chifley Labor Government and Sir Victor Hurley, from the Royal Melbourne, representing the British Medical Association (later the Australian Medical Association). The study door closed firmly on their deliberations, but I knew that they had come to talk about the Labor Party plan to nationalise medicine, which was agitating the medical profession. All I can remember is the hats they left in the hall: a black homburg for Sir Victor, and Senator McKenna's grey felt.

Kew Hill, or Vatican Hill, as it was sometimes called, was a little bubble of unreality for its Catholic families. I never heard the derogatory term 'Mick'. When one of the girls brought to school a copy of a sensational anti-Catholic journal called *The Rock* we thought its fantasies of the sex lives of nuns, with secret tunnels between convents and seminaries, were richly comic. Two or more generations of education separated my parents from whatever privations their Irish forebears must have experienced. The stories of the Irish diaspora were known only in outline, and with the emphasis on achievement, not deprivation.

Two, or perhaps three, of our four great-grandfathers emigrated from nineteenth-century Ireland as needy labourers. John Maguire went to Liverpool, worked in a match factory, and in an exemplary Horatio Alger success story, became joint owner of Maguire and Paterson, The Friendly Match, with factories in Liverpool and Belfast. His son, our great-uncle Bert, lobbied for industrial safety against the use of phosphorus (which gave the workers 'fossy-jaw') and was knighted for having braved German U-boats during the First World War to buy timber for the British Government in Japan. As Sir Alexander Herbert Maguire (still Bert at home) he fulfilled the exile's dream in a triumphant return to Ireland. He bought a big estate, complete with a private chapel and a resident chaplain, and interested himself in racing. The photograph of his horse Workman, winner of the Grand National, adorned the Christmas card he sent us in 1939, the year of that big win. His sister was my maternal grandmother.

Less spectacular but very solid was the achievement of great-grandfather John Gorman, who came from County Limerick in 1829 at the age of ten. His parents Patrick and Mary Gorman had their passages to Australia paid by Sylvester Browne (father of author 'Rolf Boldrewood') and prospered in the gold-rush period when Patrick carried provisions to the diggings. John Gorman was an early settler at Avenel, Victoria, and later in the Riverina district near Savernake where he placed seven of his nine sons in the 1870s. My mother Mary Constance Gorman, fifth of the seven children of Richard Gorman and Agnes Maguire, grew up on one of these properties, Galtee Park, near Berrigan, New South Wales.[1]

Great-grandfather John O'Connor (yet another John) was a labourer in the Euroa district of Victoria who died young, as did his wife, leaving two penniless daughters. One of the two, my paternal grandmother Annie, was lucky enough to be rescued by her clever cousins, the Flynns, who had found the way to advancement through primary school teaching. The youngest cousin, Julia Flynn, was the first woman to be Chief Inspector of Schools in Victoria.

The fourth great-grandfather, John Niall, had education and some capital when he brought his six motherless children from County Clare for reasons no one can discover. He bought the Melbourne pub, the Nag's Head, and lived very comfortably on this and other investments until the financial crash of the 1890s. This sent his book-loving son Michael to work for the first time, at the age of forty-four. As a clerk in the Lands Department he met and married twenty-six-year-old Annie O'Connor, with whom he had five sons. Her passion to place the boys in the professions was backed by Julia Flynn's expert advice. On small means, the five Niall boys went to Xavier (the family having moved to Kew for the purpose) and as each one found his place, he helped the next. Three doctors, all in Collins Street specialist practice, a lawyer and an estate agent, also practising in Collins Street, made a formidable close-knit team. The eldest, Frank Niall, was my father.

This concentration of talent in the professions was a safeguard, presumably chosen for its guarantee of independence. The common background of Irish poverty and oppression, unknown to my generation, remote to my parents, must nevertheless have contributed to the family's choices. My nine uncles were all self-employed: four doctors, one lawyer, an estate agent and three graziers. The uncles on the land—my mother's brothers—had a hard time during the Depression, but the enemy was drought, not freemasonry. None of them was vulnerable to the dismissals on sectarian grounds that were common outside our privileged little world. I knew that there were firms that wouldn't employ Catholics, and that mixed marriages were unwise though not actually wrong, but I had no sense of the suspicion and antagonism that existed in twentieth-century Australia. It seems to have gone beyond religious and class differences to a perception of the Irish that was essentially racist.

Donald Horne, a teacher's son, recalled his 1920s childhood in a New South Wales country town: 'My school friends and I believed that the 250-or-so Catholic boys and girls who went to the convent were different physically from us. Their faces were coarser than ours—more like apes.'[2] Historian Inga Clendinnen grew up in 1930s Geelong with similar stereotypes:

> For my mother, for her sisters, for almost everyone else who ever mentioned them, Catholics were as identifiable as they were reprehensible. They were

> reprehensible because they had sold themselves to a foreign power; they took their orders from the Pope, who was an Eye-tie. On his orders they bred like rabbits so they could take over the whole public service and look after their own ... But luckily you could always pick them: their eyes were set too close together and they couldn't look you in the face. The dead give-away was that they said haitch instead of aitch.[3]

Clendinnen writes about a working-class district, but racist contempt for the Irish-Australians cut across class. 'I would rather my daughter married an Aborigine' was the response of one wealthy WASP in the 1950s when a personable, well-to-do young Catholic came courting. Did Australian Catholics have similar stereotypes of Anglicans or Presbyterians? Apart from the Masonic handshake, it's hard to think how any religious grouping within the white, Anglo-Saxon Protestant majority could be identified by any physical sign, real or imagined. The litany of Irish Catholic names in our little stretch of territory in Studley Park may well have upset our non-Catholic neighbours. But prosperity seemed to go with polite behaviour: in Robert Frost's ambiguous line, 'good fences make good neighbors'.

We took our predictable world for granted, because we did not know anything else. It was a totally enclosed environment. From Catholic obstetrician to undertaker we needed no alien hands. For the children of my time it had many charms, not least to feel welcome in one another's houses, and to be free to play in the open spaces of the Yarra Bend parkland. As a community it didn't lack human variety; it had its eccentric and wayward members, its talented and creative people, its comedies and tragedies. It had the warmth and friendliness of a group where everyone knew everyone; and over the years its friendships lasted well. It was so safe that parents asked only that we be home by five o'clock. Our house was not locked until last thing at night, and none of us, except my mother, carried or possessed a key. And yet the open doors were illusory. There were invisible fences dividing us from our neighbours, and a large and varied world outside, whose existence, in that sequestered time, we did not know.

2

First Lessons

I look back at my schooldays with affection for much that was good, wonder that such a time and place existed, regret that it was so enclosed and limited, and astonishment that so many of us survived its system to live happily in a much changed world. At Genazzano, the picturesque Victorian Gothic convent in Cotham Road, Kew, designed in the 1880s by William Wardell, and exquisitely maintained, a small school was staffed by a community of about twenty nuns of the order of the Faithful Companions of Jesus. The order, originally French, was ruled from its Mother House at Broadstairs, Kent. Rapidly becoming Irish-Australian, the school retained a few touches of its European origins. One very old French nun, Mère Angèle, was rumoured to have eaten horse during the siege of Paris in 1870. A German nun, very nearly as ancient, was said to have come from a Prussian military family. She was known as Mère Philomène, which seems punitive, although Mutter Filomena might have provoked schoolgirl giggles. Mother Euphrasia was very English, Mother Angela very Irish, but the rest were mainly Australian born.

Unlike the Sisters of Mercy or Charity, this was an enclosed order. The nuns did not go home to their families nor did they visit any private house, theatre, cinema or concert hall. Nuns of other orders might be seen in shops. Not the FCJs, and only rarely with special permission, as for a medical appointment, could they be seen on trams. Always in pairs, in full habit, down to the black gloves and rosary beads, maintaining downcast eyes and bowing their heads whenever they passed a Catholic Church, they must have looked as mysterious to many non-Catholics as they were unremarkable to us.

The school had one radio, reserved for educational purposes. It was understood that Reverend Mother read the newspapers, and told her community all they needed to know. A small parlour known as the Telephone Room held the only link to the outside world. One nun, Mother Columba, was designated to make and receive calls on behalf of Reverend Mother who would lift the receiver only in extreme circumstances. None of the nuns had Australian degrees or teacher training. After the novitiate years they were sent to Switzerland or Belgium; and when world wars made Europe unreachable they went to Canada. It was a bit odd to be prepared for Matriculation in Melbourne by nuns who had never seen Melbourne University, but convents in those days were full of such contradictions that their pupils never noticed. The annual school play was given its final professional polish by Maie Hoban of the Pilgrim Theatre, who taught Elocution, but the production was the work of ebullient Mother Angela whose theatre-going, if she ever had any, would have stopped when she entered the convent in Ireland before the First World War. Nevertheless, the standard was high, at least in my last two years when the leading roles were played by the talented Mary Parker who went on to professional stage, film and TV success in London and a brief, sparkling career with Melbourne's Channel Seven, before her marriage.

The quality of teaching was patchy, very good in languages, good in English, interesting if eccentric in European history, and amateurish in science and mathematics. This unevenness did not matter so long as the girls were being prepared for the only vocations then thought possible: we were all destined to be nuns or mothers. We might think of a job, but it would not be serious; it would fill in the few years before marriage. A few under-paid middle-aged lay teachers on the convent staff gave a rather depressing image of the single woman's life. Until my last year at school when the sudden death of the science mistress prompted a quick replacement by a Mr Bennett, there were no men to be seen except Vic the gardener. His postwar successor, Mr Van Raay, arrived from Holland soon after I left school.

Mr Hay, who taught physical culture in the Concert Hall in the last period on Friday afternoons, never entered the main part of the school. Both time and place and the unpopularity of his lessons made him seem marginal. The priests who came to say morning mass or hear confessions were received with deference, and given a good breakfast or afternoon tea in solitary state in one of the parlours. The nuns disappeared for their meals, and we never saw them eat or drink.

The division between the seen and the unseen, the daily and the numinous, was expressed in the structure of the school, by the mystery of the nuns' quarters, shut off from the life of the pupils, and by the naming and distinctive qualities of each room. Schooling began in Bethlehem, which had a dolls' house in one corner and in another a cupboard full of small musical instruments, miniature drums, bells and triangles. St Anne's and St Augustine's classrooms for older girls had glass-fronted bookcases on either side of a very small fireplace, which gave little warmth to those in the back row. The youngest boarders slept in the Holy Angels dormitory; older ones in the Sacred Heart. Somewhere between these dormitories, it was said, the convent ghost, the Grey Lady, occasionally walked and wept. Reverend Mother received visitors in St Stanislaus' Parlour. There were three staircases. The grandeur of the front stairs was in sharp contrast to the narrow, homely back stairs whose worn steps linked the cellars and kitchens with the Refectory. From the uppermost stretch of the tower stairs, we were sometimes allowed to climb through a trapdoor to the rooftop where from the small platform of the bell tower we could look across Melbourne. In the grounds, a cypress walk, a rose garden and a stone grotto framing a statue of Our Lady of Lourdes added an element of the picturesque to the tennis courts, hockey field and the unkempt paddocks beyond them. We had plays and concerts, feasts and processions, countless small pious practices, prayers and music which ranged from the magnificence of psalms and plainsong to such vapid pieces as the hymn to Our Lady of Good Counsel with its dismal refrain.

> In thy guidance tranquilly reposing
> Now I face life's cares and woes anew
> O all through life and at its awful closing
> Mother, tell me what am I to do!

One early memory suggests the school's moral tone. Aged seven, I was in grade three, and very pleased to be cast in the nativity play which began with an annunciation scene. I was the smallest angel—not a starring role, but better than being a shepherd in a brown woolly garment on a hot December day. I went home to break the news to my mother that she had to make me a pair of wings, pink and silver, as gauzy and pretty as possible. My mother was not at all pleased by this happy announcement: she had no idea how to make wings. But there was someone in the family with the talent needed, and soon my mother's sister got busy and produced a quite dazzling pair, which I took to school with great pride and pleasure.

They got a mixed reception. Mother Mary de Sales thought they were wonderful, BUT—a very big BUT—they were too good for the smallest angel. Would I be a good unselfish child and give them to the Archangel Gabriel? The part of the Archangel was being played by the tallest girl in Grade Four, and the wings her mother had produced were really not up to the part. So we had to swap wings. I am sure my aunt was annoyed; I know my mother was, though she didn't openly attack the decision. An impatient sigh and a fatalistic 'Nuns are always like that' was usually as far as she would go. At the time I didn't think about the impact on the household of the Archangel Gabriel, but her mother too must have had mixed feelings when her efforts at wing-making were demoted as only good enough for the smallest angel. I felt rebuffed: as though it had been wrong to think of looking wonderful on stage in those exquisite wings.

I can now see the viewpoint of the nun whose artistic sense was affronted by the lopsided effect of the two pairs of wings. Fra Angelico wouldn't have liked it either. But what I understood from this episode and from other experiences of that kind was the importance of being unselfish, of not making a fuss when you didn't get the best or biggest pair of wings, or when you had them removed. Take it a bit further and you could read the story of the angel's wings as being against aspiration—against high flyers. Submissiveness—being good, not making a fuss—

was being confused with unselfishness. It wasn't a matter of sharing my wings, or giving to the needy: it seemed unfair; and to be praised for not protesting was not a good thing. What was later called assertiveness would in my time at school have been called boldness, or 'looking for notice', and considered very bad. You learned not to be noticed; not to argue, not to put an individual point of view. The supposedly feminine virtues of quietness and gentleness were supreme.

An equally deflating episode at about the same time as the angels' wings reversal was the music mistress's verdict on my singing voice. It was not a matter of joining a choir; it was assumed that everyone would be on stage to sing on public occasions. Called to the piano for a two-minute audition, which I failed, I was told just to mouth the words in the school concert. If I actually emitted a sound it would be out of tune and would spoil things for everyone else. I took this to heart, and never sang again at school, except in something really noisy like 'Faith of our Fathers', where it wouldn't matter. As with the nativity play, the individual—one or two tuneless seven-year-olds out of twenty—learned to defer to the general good or, in this case, the general harmony.

Silenced on stage, deprived of my wings, it was clear that I wasn't meant to be a performer. We didn't have debating classes and because I missed so many school-days I was too unreliable for any small speaking part in the annual play—not even a line like 'The guests are arriving, Your Majesty' which was usually entrusted to the dramatically challenged. Was I really the only child in the school's history ever to miss her First Communion day? That's what I was told, after a bout of bronchitis kept me from the long-planned day with the whole class, all in our white silk dresses and white veils. Six weeks later I was given my first communion, not on any ordinary morning by the parish priest, but on the next major feast day and by Archbishop Mannix himself. It was a great honour, Reverend Mother said, very pleased with herself for having arranged it, but for me it was terrifying, not so much because of the archbishop, but because of the added ritual, the splendid vestments, the full school choir, which his presence demanded. With the whole school and all the nuns in chapel for the occasion, I went through the ceremony, rigid with fear, intent only on not making a mistake when everything had to be perfect, and missing the sustaining presence of the class of seven-year-olds.

Unwanted privileges like this one could have made me an outsider at school; but my parents made a good move in taking me out of school for a year. I re-entered in fourth grade, no longer the smallest in the class, but with girls of my own age or younger. Reading skills that drew gasps of incredulity in a three-year-old were not remarkable at nine; and our farm holidays of this period changed my indoor, bookish image. With this fresh start, I found a place for myself, and made strong and lasting friendships. I still missed several weeks of school every term but I could drop out and in again, confident of my place in a clever, spirited and amusing group of girls. Within the group the Parker twins, Mary and Susan, set an example of non-conformity, not just because they were unusually gifted in art and music, but because their garden adjoined the school paddock and they could stroll in at the last minute without hats or gloves.

The kindness and warmth of most of the nuns somehow coexisted with the rigidity of their rule. The uniform black bonnets and habits didn't stifle personal quirks and foibles. Exuberant Mother Bernadette, who had a high sense of drama, was in complete contrast with tall, pale Mother Euphemia, within whose understated style was a dry ironic wit. Already an observer at nine or ten, I noted their distinctive ways. The small ceremonies and eccentricities of a highly ritualised school routine, and the formal beauty of the convent building, made a rich experience, though not what one would choose as preparation for a confident, independent life in the mid-twentieth century.

Genazzano is one of four private schools brilliantly scrutinised in Janet McCalman's *Journeyings* (to which I contributed some memories under the pseudonym 'Elinor Doyle'). Comparisons with Methodist Ladies' College show many resemblances. The convent had no monopoly on strict discipline and low aspirations in academic achievement for girls. Yet where 60 per cent of the MLC respondents to McCalman's questionnaire saw themselves as having had 'adequate self-confidence' at school, Genazzano's score was significantly lower, at only 40 per cent.[1] This difference emerges despite the fact that Genazzano girls, in McCalman's findings, were more socially adept than their Methodist contemporaries. Well schooled in deference, we had no experience in expressing differences of opinion. It was no use taking your doubts to religious knowledge classes. Questioning Sheehan's *Apologetics and Catholic Doctrine* was a serious matter; it was presumption, an offshoot of pride. When one of my classmates was rebuked for inattention during a homily from the parish priest, she unwisely defended herself: 'But, Mother, he's so dull!' This turned out not only to be a breach of courtesy, but to transgress the second commandment, by failing 'to speak with reverence of God and of holy persons and things'. I doubt if many of us took this interpretation of the catechism too seriously, but we learned not to express dissent.

Genazzano's religious training was inward-looking, intent on the salvation of the soul; and though the catechism told us that faith without good works was not enough, we did not hear much about the world in which work should be done. Sins against truthfulness and kindness were taken seriously, but concern for our neighbours' welfare was a vague aspiration. The poverty and unemployment in those Depression years were never, in my memory, discussed at school, although a little group of men outside the kitchen door, waiting to be given a hot meal by Sister Joan, showed the nuns' readiness to give practical help. Charity, rather than social justice, was the lesson we learned.

At home, my parents' worries about the Depression reached me piecemeal, as things happened. Sad men came to the door with suitcases that they opened to reveal shoelaces and other small unwanted objects which my mother always bought. She thought it was wrong to put a No Hawkers sign on the gate, and she was very scornful about a well-off acquaintance whose response to the economic crisis was to 'do without' one of her two maids and claim it as a virtue. She was shaken and distressed when our maid Millie, who had been with us for only a month or so, was found to be stealing and had to be dismissed (or as the euphemism had it,'let go'.) At eight or nine years old, I was round-eyed with wonder at this event. I knew the ten commandments but hadn't thought to get so close to one of the big ones. My mother responded unexpectedly and quite sharply to my questions: 'Don't think you could never steal because you could. Anyone could.' She cheered up when she found that Millie had made an unrepentantly thorough job of clearing her room, taking the sheets and towels in the suitcase which my brother John carried to the tram for her, because it was so heavy.

My mother had not seen poverty during her country childhood, nor in the first years of her marriage. She had a sharp awakening in 1929 in Vienna where my father studied for a time after passing his London postgraduate exams. One story, which haunted her, was that of a wonderful evening at the Vienna Opera House, after which, elated by the experience, she and my father decided to walk back to their hotel. It was winter; there were beggars outside the Opera House, and homeless men sleeping in doorways. Back at the hotel, outside their room, a little girl, perhaps twelve years old at most, was half-asleep on an upright chair, having been told to wait in case these guests wanted a hot drink or anything else. They gave her a large tip and sent her to bed, but remained troubled by the episode.

My father had an unshielded view of the privations of the time. Much of his week's work was with the poor of Fitzroy in his public wards at St Vincent's; and he gave them the same attention as his private patients, including unscheduled weekend visits. This work, which was unpaid and demanding, eased my mother's social conscience to some extent, and perhaps his too, though I think he found the hospital rounds and clinical teaching (also unpaid) too absorbing to count them as public service. Both parents did their best to be good employers in those Depression years and they employed rather more help than was needed. As well as the live-in cook-general, we had a morning housemaid five days a week, someone to wash and iron on Mondays, and a gardener-handyman two days a week. When the Second World War virtually put an end to domestic service by calling women to the munitions factories, we owned our kitchen for the first time; and we could linger over dinner without feeling guiltily aware that the maid was waiting to wash the dishes and finish her day's work. We never again had live-in help, and very little by the day. We did, however, get a magnificent Dishlex, one of the very first dishwashers, soon after the end of the war.

The small uncertainties of home, with its glimpses of insoluble problems, were not matched in school life, where doubt never entered. Discipline was not particularly strict, or at least it did not appear to be so. Classes were small and the nuns were so perfectly in control of an elaborately mannered system that open defiance almost never happened. And because of that control, they were usually able to appear as calm and gentle as they wanted their pupils to be. The rule of the order forbade physical punishment but there were subtler means. Icy sarcasm or ridicule were not uncommon. Out of many incidents, one well-remembered story. One of the half-dozen boys admitted to the first two years of school was David Falkland, who sat next to me in the classroom known as Bethlehem. One day, six-year-old David slipped into the junior cloakroom where one of the boarders had left her new Sunday hat, a magnificent affair, trimmed with ribbons, lace ruffles, flowers and cherries. David dropped the hat, head downwards, into one of the circular tip-up marble wash basins and turned on the tap. Later when the sodden, ruined hat was retrieved, David was punished, not by being kept in, or sent home, or sent to Reverend Mother for a personal reprimand, but by being made to sit all day in the corridor, wearing this deplorable hat, for the whole school to see.

Our progress in morals and manners was monitored every week by an elaborate system known as Marks. Lapses were measured by deductions from a notional score of three under the headings of Silence, Order, Exactitude, Application, Deportment, Courtesy and Conduct. To lose more than three meant the public shame of not being noticed by Reverend Mother at the weekly ceremony which took place before the whole school. If your name was called, with a 'No Marks Lost', you stood up, bowed, and got an approving nod. One for Silence —probably for talking in the ranks—was not too bad. An untidy desk or a hole in your glove would lose One for Order. No use to say that your tram was late: that would be One for Exactitude. Deportment might be for whistling, or failing to stand when a nun entered the room. Courtesy was the same as Deportment, but more serious, while Conduct was for something so appalling that none of us knew how it could be merited. This was Expulsion territory, and I can't remember that anyone was expelled in my time. The interesting twist of the Marks system was that wickedness (more than a total of three lost marks) was punished by being publicly ignored. Your name was not read out, and you remained seated. Any nun, or any lay teacher, could record your lapse. This power extended even to members of an anonymous group known as 'kind friends of the school'. These vigilantes—usually past pupils—travelled incessantly on public transport. They might report you for rudeness to a tram conductor (not saying thank you) or failing to stand up for an adult. Kind friends even lurked outside Lilley's Milk Bar, near the Glenferrie Road tram stop, where a few words with a Xavier boy meant real trouble, unless he happened to be your brother, which was not usually the case.

Other convents had similar schemes of discipline, but the precise details of Marks were peculiar to the FCJ order, and observed internationally, in all its convents.

Kate O'Brien's novel *The Land of Spices*, set between 1906 and 1914 in the FCJ convent of Laurel Hill, Limerick, describes a Marks ceremony identical with that of Genazzano in 1948. When I told Mother Angela, who had been at Laurel Hill in O'Brien's time, that I had discovered a novel about her old school, she said wistfully that she would love to read it. But 'we are told there is a bad page in it'. Indeed there was, but because it was a homosexual episode, obliquely described in half a sentence, I hadn't fully understood it. Entranced by the familiar world of the Irish convent, encountering for the first time a novel which presented attitudes, manners and customs so like our own, I didn't register the fact that this was O'Brien's backward glance at schooldays which ended just before the First World War. Because so little had changed in our hermetically sealed world of school, it was real, while *Dimsie Among the Prefects* and other English boarding-school sagas, to which I was addicted, were fantasy.

The Land of Spices, which I discovered in the adult section of the Mornington Lending Library, was my first experience of a novel in which Catholic religious belief was central, and taken for granted. I don't remember any other books about Catholic children—certainly not about Australian Catholic children. In an odd reversal of our everyday total immersion in Catholicism, all the children's books we read were Protestant. I learned about Presbyterians and Methodists from *Anne of Green Gables* and its successors, in which the children of the manse had major roles. The Billabong books were Church of England in a low-key way, with a few Irish characters whose social inferiority was balanced by an innate 'cheeriness'. The *Catholic School Paper* ran some pious serials so feeble that I didn't read them. At home we had Chesterton's Father Brown stories, *The Man Who Was Thursday* and *The Napoleon of Notting Hill.* My mother looked a bit doubtful when she noticed me reading her copy of *Brideshead Revisited*, and said that I might enjoy it more when I was older. But I was enjoying it already. The florid prose which Waugh later disdained was just right for a fifteen-year-old, even though the homosexual relationships were still puzzling.

At seventeen, during my last year at school, I read most of Graham Greene; and had just finished *The Heart of the Matter* when it was denounced from the pulpit at the Sacred Heart Church, Kew. This novel was promptly placed off limits for the Matriculation class at Genazzano. Assuming a look of innocent confusion, I admitted having already read it. This was awkward for the class mistress. Had I my parents' permission? Yes, I had. And they had both read it, I added, cutting off her line of escape. 'In that case', said Mother Mary Philomena, 'if your parents think you are sufficiently mature ... BUT the rest of you are NOT to read it.' I didn't think then of the awkwardness of her situation. This very intelligent woman, a gifted teacher of Shakespeare and the Victorian novel, was not allowed to read any of the modern books from which she had to protect her pupils. Her warnings, in that final year of school, about the moral and intellectual perils of Melbourne University were likewise based on hearsay of the vaguest kind. Other teaching orders, such as the Brigidines, or the Presentation nuns (who taught Germaine Greer) had more windows to the world than the FCJs of my time. Until the 1960s the FCJ rule reflected many of the social and educational presuppositions of its foundress, Marie Madeleine d'Houet, who was a child at the time of the French Revolution. After the changes in the Catholic Church brought about by the Second Vatican Council, the rules of this enclosed order was modified. Its nuns now do welfare work in South East Asia, and lay teachers run a much enlarged school. Today's new buildings almost overwhelm Wardell's Victorian Gothic convent, which in my time encompassed boarding and day school and religious community, all in one.

Rebellious feelings simmered but were seldom expressed in this hothouse of religious and social convention. Ambition—worldly ambition as we would have called it—was equally rare. It may have been easier for me to get high marks in my last year because it really didn't matter one way or the other. My teachers had no ideas to offer. My parents were still overprotective, even though asthma was now only a minor problem. To be left free to study or not, as I pleased, was not entirely a bad thing. The time for idling—and I had lots of that—was valuable too. I suspect that the leisurely evenings I spent listening to trashy radio serials, or reading widely and at random, would these days be divided up into study periods and dedicated to assignments, music practice and sports training. Today's insistence on high achievement in everything must be daunting.

Because it was such an uncompetitive atmosphere I wasn't expecting my success in the last year at school. In the Matriculation exam—today's VCE—I shared the exhibition in English Literature and with four first-class honours was placed among the top thirty students in the state. Recently I found the newspaper cutting which gave the results, and studied the names of the other twenty-nine. There were three girls and twenty-six boys. I don't know what became of the other girls. Among the boys there were some now familiar names of high achievers: James Gobbo, a Rhodes Scholar who became Governor of Victoria, and Gerald O'Collins, a Jesuit priest who has a major post at the Vatican. Predictably the boys' private schools dominated the list. In that 1948 group, Scotch had six winners, and the rest were spread among Wesley, Xavier, Melbourne Grammar, Geelong Grammar. The selective government schools for boys, University High School and Melbourne High School, were represented. There was one winner from each of four girls' schools: Presbyterian Ladies' College, Methodist Ladies' College, Firbank and Genazzano. And one solitary boy from Upwey High—I wonder what happened to him.

Of course boys were programmed, as girls were, but to a different model. My brothers were all-rounders who could have done anything. Much to my envy, they left the Xavier platform on Speech Night with more gold-monogrammed books for their well-endowed prizes than they could easily carry. Each of them accumulated a dozen or so volumes of the English poets, in the handsome Oxford edition, on fine paper with dark blue covers. Hugh, who was even allowed to choose his own prizes in his last year, added Wodehouse and Sherlock Holmes to his stack of classics. The Jesuits had no problems with competitiveness and demonstrable success. But if the boys had wanted to do anything other than medicine or law, I think they'd have had some very frosty looks from the priests, and some uneasiness, at best, from our parents. Is it like that these days for girls too, I wonder? If you can get a place in these competitive fields, is it easy to refuse? That may be the downside of a stronger focus on achievement than was there for women of my time.

At my last school assembly, in 1948, I'd looked forward to getting the only two subject prizes awarded in the Matriculation year. With first place in both of them, for English and French, it was a certainty. However, the English prize went to the girl who came second. Mystified, I asked what had happened. It had been decided, I was told, that no one should have more than one prize; and because I'd won the English prize the year before, this was my turn for French. So, once more, academic achievement was confusingly entangled in moral development. Subject prizes were far outnumbered by prizes for General Satisfaction, Courtesy, Devotedness, Order, Loyalty, Good Spirit and Early and Regular

Attendance—all stressing the domestic virtues. I didn't win any of those. My French prize was a peculiarly ugly and unreadable book about nature study, with smudgy photographs of kangaroos and wombats. Printed on the yellowish austerity paper that had been used in wartime it was almost certainly not bought for the occasion. I was so disgusted that I transferred the inscribed sticker to something that at least looked like a prize for French. This was a handsome copy of *Paul et Virginie*, found at home, in mint condition, probably because someone had bought it by mistake, not noticing that it was in French. A decorative item on my bookshelves, it was a fraud which gave me no pleasure. Some years later my sister Margaret came home with an even more obnoxious volume than my nature book. In our private contest for Genazzano's worst, Margaret's *Edel Quin: a Heroine of the Apostolate* was the undoubted winner. When educationists in later times argued for the abolition of the concept of failure, I thought of Genazzano. The nuns had no problem with failing their students: they did it all the time. It was success that troubled them.

It was assumed at home and at school that I would do Arts at Melbourne University, but there was little or no discussion about whatever might come next. My older sister, Philippa, followed her arts degree with a diploma in librarianship and worked at the State Library until her marriage. I didn't want an identical career; I wasn't attracted by teaching; and it was hard to think of anything else. Of the sixteen girls in my Matriculation class, only eight sat and passed. The rest, all highly intelligent and capable of anything they wanted to do, either didn't sit, or just picked up a subject or two. Several had been rendered ineligible to matriculate by failing in chemistry the year before. In most schools, a 75 per cent failure rate would have caused concern. Not at Genazzano, where it reinforced the idea that girls were not meant for science, nor for any career. Out of those who did take up a profession, I can think of only one who continued after marriage as a matter of course, though several returned after an interval. Home and family turned out well and happily for nearly everyone, but it could not be said that any of us was making a real choice. When one girl from my class, widowed very young, went back to teaching, it was said, in a revealing but predictable comment: what a good thing she had that to fall back on! The teaching profession did not then welcome married women. Teachers in state schools, like public servants at that time, were made to resign when they married. Private schools could employ married women but seldom did, except in wartime.

I left Genazzano in 1948, nearly thirty years after my mother ended her schooldays there. This made for an extraordinary continuity. Nuns who had taught my mother, my aunt and various older cousins were still there, perhaps showing a few wrinkles beneath the black bonnet but unchanged in ideas and classroom style. Old Mother Mary, who found me looking tearful on my first morning, and broke the rules by taking me into the nuns' common room to give me chocolate money from her desk, had been equally kind to my mother in 1914. In 1936, as the order's Mother Vicar, she outranked Reverend Mother, and so could breach convent discipline to console one of the school's 'granddaughters', as this second generation was called. The drawback of this family feeling was the expectation of sameness, if not improvement, on the earlier generation. I was expected to be quiet, shy and clever, like my mother, and to give no trouble, except for the chance of an asthma attack. Reasoning that I might as well get some advantage from an unwelcome ailment, I exploited the nuns' anxiety about my health by dodging physical culture and sport. Inexplicably, the nuns overlooked my refusal, for several years, to do any needlework. They deferred to my father ('your dear father'), who was credited with saving the lives of several members of the community. He would not have approved my taking these exemptions but because he was never asked nor told, I kept my unwarranted privileges. Comforting or constricting? The school was both, and so was the suburb of Kew within whose large Catholic community my family as well as the school was enclosed.

In my earliest years, there was one non-Catholic girl in my class. She could have been Anglican, Presbyterian or Baptist: we would never ask, nor be much interested. She was best known for making an occasion for a special lecture after bad behaviour of some kind. Mother Emmanuel started proceedings by sending her out of the room. 'Coralie, dear, would you get your little case from the cloakroom for me?' Bewildered Coralie (whose name was actually Corelle) complied. In her three minutes of absence, Mother Emmanuel gave her rebuke, adding to our disgrace the fact that we had '*behaved badly in front of a little non-Catholic girl*'. Corelle returned; her little case was pronounced very nice; and, unenlightened about this weird performance, she was sent back to the cloakroom to restore the case. We knew that it was important to show non-Catholics a good example, but with few opportunities in our segregated life, we had to do our best with Corelle. It was also important to be especially polite to tram conductors: non-Catholics would notice bad behaviour on public transport and be scandalised.

For the Catholic daughters of a mixed marriage, Religious Knowledge lessons were uncomfortable, perhaps terrifying. Could their non-Catholic parent go to heaven? Well, yes, provided he or she lived a good life. But anyone who wilfully turned aside from the enlightenment offered by the Church would be in trouble. On the whole it seemed safer never to have had the chance of instruction. Keeping Catholics and non-Catholics apart was the best way. A mixed marriage was difficult, given the non-negotiable demand that the children be brought up in the Catholic faith. Nevertheless, it wasn't quite ruled out. In an unguarded moment, outside the classroom, Mother Angela offered a concession: 'If you were thirty, and it was your last chance, the Lord probably wouldn't mind very much'. The ban on divorce was absolute, but because we would never have expected to meet a divorced man it was not discussed.

It would be easy to dismiss this eccentric convent education as entirely anachronistic and absurd. It wasn't. Guaranteeing fine weather for a hockey match by putting the statue of St Joseph out in the rain was a quaint custom: no one believed in it, least of all the nuns. The prizes for politeness and penalties for lost gloves over-emphasised order but didn't suppress individualism. In an atmosphere that discouraged cliques there was no playground bullying and very little teasing. The friendships I made in my first years at Genazzano are still strong today. If there was too much emphasis on standing back, giving up and keeping quiet, it went with an alertness to the rights and feelings of others. The nuns' belief in their self-denying vocation was real. Mother Mary Philomena meant it when she gave the readings in chapel on Fridays: 'I live now, not I, but Christ liveth in me'. The formal beauty of much of the liturgy was satisfying. The music of *O Salutaris* and *Tantum Ergo* at Benediction made up for some insipid hymns, as did the enduring mystery and poetry of the litany of the Blessed Virgin: 'Tower of Ivory, House of Gold, Ark of the Covenant, Mystical Rose, Morning Star, Gate of Heaven'.

Moving on to the University of Melbourne should have enlarged my world but it did so in very small and tentative ways. The Newman Society, in which many Catholic girls found their social life and future husbands, provided another cocoon. The honours arts degree, for which I enrolled in the Department of English, was then completed in only three years. Because I was diffident and slow to settle in, my first year was almost an extension of school days, except for the excitement of discovering Donne, Vaughan and Herbert, Yeats and Eliot, and hearing *The Waste Land* so superbly read by Ian Maxwell, then head of the English Department, that I went back to his evening lecture to hear it again. I began to enjoy myself in second year. I had learned by then the workings of the Dewey system which was unknown at Genazzano, or not needed because one small glass-fronted bookcase contained all the reference books. Tutorials, where you had to volunteer opinions, were becoming less threatening, and my circle of friends even included a few non-Catholics.

Discovering the newly opened Department of Fine Arts, I dropped my sub-major in History in order to do Joseph Burke's wonderful course in eighteenth-century art, architecture and landscape gardening. In the second-year exams of the School of English I won first place and two prizes. Finals looked promising. At home we talked about my going to Oxford. This was an enticing prospect, although I had no ambitions for an academic career. Even in the Arts Faculty, female role models were scarce. I liked Miss Vera Jennings of the English Department, but her lectures were embarrassingly bad, poorly organised, rambling, and at times inaudible. It was an appalling waste to let her lecture, week after week, on Shakespeare. The History Department's Kathleen Fitzpatrick was another matter. The hem of Miss Jennings' pastel floral skirt drooped unevenly beneath her black academic gown. Mrs (later Associate Professor) Fitzpatrick, in a severely cut black dress, dramatised her gown with a single piece of jewellery: usually a sapphire brooch that accentuated her deep blue eyes. Added to that, an intelligent and perfectly structured lecture, delivered with an actor's timing, made her an unreachable model of professional ease, while Miss Jennings was a warning of the depths of female incompetence.

Would I have taken the chance of Oxford? When it was discussed during the summer before I started finals it seemed more than likely. I had three friends who were already choosing their Oxford colleges, and a fourth who was to study in Paris. My finals year, however, began with the collapse of our small, safe world. University life, which seemed scarcely to have started, became irrelevant to the larger concerns at home. My father, then aged fifty-two, at the height of his powers as a consultant cardiologist and clinical teacher, developed a brain tumour from which he died a year later. Thus, at an age when I should have been moving out to an enlarged experience of life, I became almost totally (and I now think self-protectively) involved in home and family concerns. My mother's stoicism as she faced widowhood at the age of forty-nine, with three school-age children—the youngest only six—masked desolation and panic.

Forcing themselves to meet the worst, my parents sold the big Studley Park Road house, and invested the profits. Our Mornington house was leased, and sold a year or two later. Arrangements were also made to sell the medical practice on terms, over a number of years, to a young physician who was brought in as an assistant. The reason was kept secret, so that my father could work as long as possible. The secrecy was a burden that perhaps bore most heavily on the younger children, who were not told what was wrong but must have sensed it. This was a mistake which two normally perceptive people shouldn't have made—but under pressure my parents were not thinking normally. Philippa, who was travelling in Europe and planning to work in England, was not told until late in the year, when she was called home. John and I, the two eldest at home, told no one. John sat for finals in medicine, fully aware of both parents' hopes for his future as a specialist, which meant getting a high place in the class lists and a residency at St Vincent's—as he did.

My own situation, doing finals in Arts, seemed less serious. Confident that I could catch up quickly, I neglected university work to join in the search for a new house and the preparations for the auction at Studley Park Road. Leaving the house that represented my mother's creativity and the whole family's sense of permanence was a huge emotional wrench. Choosing carpets and curtains, supervising painters and other tradesmen at our new home—a Federation villa in Burke Road, Kew, rather shabby, with two beautiful main rooms, cramped bedroom space and an inconvenient kitchen—

was a diversion. We moved house in October: too close to my final exams in mid-November. Fluency and a good memory got me through the two-week ordeal of daily exam papers which then completed the honours degree but I was seriously underprepared for the Old and Middle English papers, and for Literary Theory and Aesthetics, in which I hadn't even enrolled for the weekly tutorials. My thesis, written in two weeks, was feeble. I disliked it so much that I didn't collect it from the English Department after the exams. I never thought of applying for special consideration; and because we were the last students to do the honours degree in three years, it seemed too difficult to defer. Joining the new four-year system, I thought, might mean two more years for me. Deferring exams till February would not help. My father's condition could only get worse, as it did: he died in March.

I knew I wouldn't get a first but wasn't quite prepared for the disappointment when the results came. I probably owed my respectable upper second class honours to the kindness of examiners who may have sensed that something was wrong with the student who had won first place in the preceding year. A postgraduate award was no consolation and in due course I wasted my two-year enrolment and dropped out. The failure to get a first was made worse by the need to pretend I didn't mind too much, and not to mention Oxford. I hadn't wept for the loss of our house, nor did I shed any tears over the class list. I had a sense that if I let myself cry over this, even in private, then the floodgates would open on all the grief of the whole family in that sad year.

It was no doubt said of my mother that she was lucky not to need to work. It might have been better if my father had not tried so hard, in the last months before his death, to provide materially for us all. Her Genazzano education hadn't prepared my mother for anything but marriage and motherhood. As a widow she had a very limited social life, as did most single women of that time. After a dinner party at which the numbers were balanced by a hard-to-find extra man, she said 'never again'. Disliking the sense of being a problem for a hostess rather than welcomed in her own right, she closed the door on my father's circle of friends. At forty-nine she was a very pretty, intelligent woman who should not have dropped out of her social life—or been dropped from it. I don't think she had many invitations. She was the more isolated because, in an extraordinary sequence of deaths, she soon lost her mother, her only sister and her two closest women friends.

There had been a huge public tribute to my father. St Patrick's Cathedral was packed door to door for a Requiem Mass, with two archbishops (Mannix and Simonds), three or four bishops and the heads of the main religious orders on the altar; and in the congregation the representatives of St Vincent's, the Royal Melbourne, the Alfred and the Prince Henry's hospitals, with many friends, former students and patients, prefects from Xavier and Genazzano, and a guard of honour of

St Vincent's nurses outside the Cathedral. It was a great occasion, but when we went home to our quiet house it was no help at all.

It happened that my graduation day at the University of Melbourne coincided with the week of my father's death. After unsuccessful surgery, he was in a coma at St Vincent's Hospital, my mother beside him, for ten days during which his family tried to present the stoic front that we all believed was right. I decided to go alone to the degree ceremony. I didn't ask for company, nor even mention the occasion at home. For years afterwards the academic procession in the Union Theatre was associated in my mind with the ordeal of the long walk down the centre aisle of St Patrick's Cathedral, past the rows of mourners, and the nurses' guard of honour. Graduation day wasn't to be the end of my university education, but for a long time I had no heart for continuing it.

3

Interviewing the Archbishop

One autumn afternoon in 1959, I am in Studley Park Road once more. I pass our house—no longer ours—and think of former neighbours. Mr Menzies has left Howard Street. Firmly ensconced in the Prime Minister's Lodge, he will be there for some time. John Wren is dead. His white colonnaded dwelling will soon belong to the Jesuits as part of the Xavier preparatory school Burke Hall. But across the road at Raheen, Archbishop Daniel Mannix lives on in the tall red brick mansion with the tower, still ruling his people at the age of ninety-five.

By chance I already know Raheen. More than once as a schoolgirl I was entrusted with a letter from Reverend Mother at Genazzano, which she inscribed 'per favour Miss Brenda Niall'. It was thought more polite to send a letter by hand than by post; and as a good reliable child guaranteed not to lose, drop or smudge the envelope, I was chosen to do the errand on my way home from school. The ritual included a glass of cordial and a slice of fruit cake, brought by the housekeeper, and a benign nod of recognition from the Archbishop. This time my role will be different. Dr Mannix is expecting me, and I am to do the first of a series of interviews for an authorised biography.

I am not yet an author. I am a biographer's research assistant. The biographer is B.A. Santamaria, Catholic intellectual and activist who in the mid-1950s suddenly became almost as famous as Mannix himself. Admiration and alarm in equal measure attend Santamaria, who since the 1940s has led a campaign against communist control of the Australian trade unions, with devastating consequences for the Australian Labor Party. In this campaign Santamaria had the backing of the Catholic bishops, particularly Archbishop Mannix. Older Australians remembered the turmoil of the First World War, when Mannix, newly arrived from Ireland, spoke out with such passion and supple wit against Prime Minister Hughes' conscription referendums that he was credited with their defeat. In the 1950s Mannix again spoke out. Even in his nineties he was formidable, and his support for Santamaria's anti-communist 'Movement'[3] was crucial. Passions had cooled just a little by 1959, but the combination of Mannix and Santamaria—the old Irish churchman and the law graduate from an Italian migrant family with an exotic name—was still explosive. Both men charmed and dazzled, divided and enraged. As public figures, both were idealised and demonised to a degree that took away their individuality.

When I was invited by Santamaria to do the research for the Mannix biography, I was flattered to be chosen and eager to understand the subject. It would by any measure be an important book: a life of one powerful man by the closest friend and associate of his last years. Just back in Australia after nearly a year overseas, I should have been thinking seriously about a career. In that decade of early marriages most of my school friends were already wives and mothers. Now, with my future so vague, it made no sense for me to immerse myself in Irish history in the company of a ninety-five-year-old archbishop. Yet that is what I had chosen when I stood on the Raheen doorstep in 1959.

From the first moments, the Mannix interviews went wrong. Seated by the fireplace in his high-backed chair, the Archbishop took charge. It was as though he was interviewing me. In his soft, beautifully modulated voice, pausing in mid-sentences, he enquired about my mother: was she well? He spoke of the Church's great debt to my father, who had looked after the health of so many religious. He knew we had left Studley Park Road. Were my younger brother and sisters still at school? He did not remind me, but I remembered his offer, after my father's death, to have their school fees at Xavier and Genazzano waived for their remaining years. My mother refused, but was pleased by his thoughtfulness. It was also of course a sign of his power. Although these two schools were independent of diocesan authority, neither would have resisted a hint from Raheen.

The Archbishop's enquiries made me conscious of the difficulty of my role. There was a certain weariness in the courtesies; and no sign that he was ready to talk about himself. Sitting opposite him, with my blank notepad open, I tried awkwardly to reverse our roles. I was naive enough to have thought that we would begin at the beginning, and from there the words would flow. There was no tape recorder. Someone who refused to speak on the telephone was not likely to allow this more recent form of technology. Recording would not have helped much; the words came so slowly and quietly that I had plenty of time to transcribe. My halting questions about his childhood drew a sentence or two, before an unmistakable full stop. The convention of indirect address made it harder. As with royalty, so with princes of the church. 'Would Your Grace tell me ... does Your Grace remember?' So it went on, from birth in Charleville, County Cork, on an unimaginably distant date of 1864, to his family, their farm, his schooling. 'Did your Grace have brothers and sisters?' Yes, he was one of eight children. Three had died in infancy. Again the full stop. I wanted to ask what happened to the others, but it would have felt like a digression from our slow progress through his life story. As for the intimate questions about family love, rivalries, ambitions, disappointments, they were almost unthinkable. It was like interviewing the Pope. And yet, for all the discrepancies in our situations, I didn't feel that the Archbishop was altogether remote from me. He knew how to wait, and how to use silences. Perhaps he was giving me a chance to make something out of our absurd tête à tête.

Things brightened a little when we reached the eight-year-old Daniel Mannix. When the Bishop came to the parish primary school, noting those who were ready for promotion to the Christian Brothers: 'I was such a big boy that the nuns hid me in a cupboard'. I wrote that down, pleased at last to have an anecdote. But it was a meagre return for our time together, and when at last the Archbishop rang for tea I felt as though I had failed in a stiff oral examination. Tea didn't help. There were two cups, but the housekeeper caught an imperceptible signal of refusal from the Archbishop and filled only one. The ritual of the silver teapot, fine china and linen napkins was all for me, as was the homemade fruit cake. It wasn't easy to manoeuvre it all under the Archbishop's gentle, silent gaze. Cup, saucer, plate, teaspoon, cake fork, milk jug, sugar tongs: I handled them as tentatively as if they had been small incendiary devices. I can't remember whether or not proceedings closed with the ordeal of the tea cup. A veteran of thousands of interviews, Mannix knew how to give the signal of dismissal. He would be glad to see me again, he said. It sounded sincere, if not enthusiastic. He had one last question for me. Did I like doing this work for Mr Santamaria? Yes, I did. It was my turn for the full stop. Absurd to tell him what an interesting life he'd had. 'It's an honour, Your Grace' was a cliché. So we matched silences and he stood up, still handsome, tall and 'straight as a Roman spear'.[1] He held out his frail, long-fingered hand (another dilemma: should I kiss his ring, or was this a gesture of blessing?) and surprised me by answering a question I would never have asked: 'I think that Mr Santamaria is the cleverest man I ever knew'.

It was the only spontaneous remark of the afternoon. The word 'cleverest' surprised me: so an old schoolmaster might have spoken of a pupil. Spoken with admiration, perhaps with pride, it reminded me that when Santamaria was born, in 1915, Mannix was fifty-one. When he singled out the twenty-two-year-old law graduate for a major role in the church, he changed his protégé's life. Some said that the Archbishop was used by the younger man as a means to power. But those who saw Santamaria as 'the son Mannix never had' seemed to be nearer the mark.

My second interview was better. We reached the years just before the First World War, when Mannix was President of Maynooth, the seminary in which the more gifted Irish priests were trained. Mannix was willing to move briefly through the issues of the time. Had he thought there should be compulsory instruction in the Irish language? No, he had not. Did all the seminarians do a university degree? Yes, he had so ruled. He had more to say on these topics, but not much more.

If prompted, the Archbishop was perfectly willing to tell me things I already knew. One of these was the famous dilemma of 1903, when Edward VII's visit to Maynooth posed a diplomatic problem. Instead of the Union Jack, which would offend Irish nationalist sensitivities, Mannix arranged for the King's racing colours to fly above the college. The King was amused, and the visit passed off smoothly. At this point I could have asked—but didn't—how Mannix felt about the playing of 'God Save the King' on public occasions in Melbourne. In my own schooldays there was at least one St Patrick's Night concert when 'God Save Ireland' was preferred 'because His Grace will be with us'.

So it went on, with the Archbishop patiently retelling the old stories, adding nothing. On my side there was a growing awareness that I was wasting a great deal of time in recording material that was already in print. This was not the first Mannix biography; and a competent researcher would have assimilated all the available sources before troubling a tired old man. I heard the account of his first day in Australia. Stepping on to the railway platform in Adelaide in 1913, he had seen the asphalt bubbling in 100 degree heat, and thought: 'I won't live a year in this climate. But, as you see, I am still here'. How many school prize nights, how many communion breakfasts, had heard the same story, and seen the same faint ironic smile?

There were other good stories, all well known. My favourite (did he repeat it, or did I only read it?) was the famous episode in 1920 when the British Government stopped Mannix from landing in Ireland to visit his ninety-year-old mother. The fear of his stirring nationalist passions in a time of armed rebellion was so great that a British Navy destroyer was sent to intercept the ship on which he was travelling from the United States. When Mannix refused the request to leave the passenger ship, the captain of the destroyer made the formal gesture of arrest. The story passed into legend with the Archbishop's comment after being deposited on English soil: 'Not since the battle of Jutland has the British navy scored a success comparable with the capture of the Archbishop of Melbourne without the loss of a single British sailor'.

More and more I felt that the afternoons at Raheen were a charade. It seemed possible that the Archbishop wanted his part in the biography to be on record. If anyone thought that at ninety-five his understanding was fading, my notes would testify that it was not. But he was not interested in revisiting his past. Someone with more experience than I possessed might have broken through and prompted some new reflection. In fact, this was done two or three years later by the ABC's Gerald Lyons whose brilliant TV interview, recorded at Raheen, showed the Archbishop's alertness to the politics of the day. In effect, I admitted defeat and turned belatedly to documentary sources. Because of the Archbishop's age, it had seemed sensible to start by talking to him, but the rewards were minimal.

Documents, too, proved elusive. At Santamaria's request, I was given an interview with Monsignor (later Bishop) Fox at St Patrick's Cathedral, where presumably there was a vast archive of Mannix material. Fox had no intention of opening the files for me. He said that Dr Mannix did not keep personal papers of any kind. I doubt if I could have made anything of the diocesan records, but clearly they were off limits. Fox made one concession. He would look around, and if there was anything that might be helpful he would send it to Raheen. He kept his promise and sent a box that I opened with high hopes. Seated at a magnificent polished mahogany table in Mannix's vast library, I searched for treasures. There were none. This was a boxful of old Christmas cards, coloured holy pictures chosen by the devout, and little notes, some in nuns' copperplate, others barely literate. All were from Melbourne parishioners, including a few priests. Most consisted of only a few words: grateful thanks, blessings and prayers: that was all I could find. No doubt each one told a story, and an ethnographer could have made something from them. I couldn't. I never knew whether to suspect the humourless Monsignor Fox of having his little joke. It was true that this was personal correspondence from Mannix's people. As for the ones I hoped to find—letters from Ireland, from his family, from old friends, from cardinals and prime ministers—there was not a scrap to show the private man.

I told Santamaria my worries. With his usual optimism, he reassured me: he was sure more material would come to light, and in the meantime he thought my work was really valuable. As always, he was embroiled in at least one crisis and his mind was not on the Mannix biography.

From time to time he found other research projects for me. One was an article he had promised to the Jesuit quarterly *Twentieth Century*, attacking the White Australia policy (which was still ALP and Liberal orthodoxy) for its racist origins and intentions. I reworked his notes, added a stanza from an anti-Chinese goldfields ballad and part of a speech by Sir Henry Parkes. The seams showed a little, but not enough to matter, and I was quite pleased with the result, which was published almost without alteration under his name.[2] The optimism with which he gave me this task, with its almost instant deadline, matched the impulsive moment, some years earlier, that had led to my involvement in the Movement.

I had first met Bob Santamaria and his beautiful and highly intelligent wife Helen at the house of our Kew neighbour, Melbourne University law lecturer Frank Maher, who had preceded Santamaria as Director of Catholic Action and remained his close friend. Over the tea cups that evening Santamaria instantly offered me a job as research assistant. This included the editorship of *Rural Life*, the monthly journal of the National Catholic Rural Movement. I knew nothing about the Rural Movement; and my only experience of Catholic Action was that of meetings at school, where we had gospel readings followed by discussions about applying the gospel to our own lives. I had usually found these meetings dull. Bob Santamaria didn't seem dull; and the idea of editing a journal was appealing.

At the time, early in 1954, I was at something of a loose end. My enrolment at Melbourne University for an

MA thesis had just expired, with almost nothing written. I had also finished my job as a part-time receptionist for the successor to my father's medical practice and for my two uncles who shared the same suite of rooms at 33 Collins Street. This was a city home base in our childhood; the place to drop in after a dentist appointment or a film matinee in the school holidays, to get a lift home, to borrow money for a milk shake or a new book, or to be taken to lunch at the Wattle Tea Rooms in Little Collins Street. The fourth Niall brother, Arthur, whose office was at 127 Collins Street, sometimes took me to lunch at the Oriental Hotel next door to 33. I started work at 33 just before my father's death, and stayed on. So long as the uncles were there, with their secretaries who were also our friends, I enjoyed the sociability of my undemanding part-time job, doing the banking and the waiting-room flowers and typing tape-recorded reports for which my skill in spelling medical terms compensated for untrained fingering.

In June 1952, three months after my father's death, came the shock of seeing Arthur collapse from a heart attack one afternoon at his brothers' rooms. He had walked up Collins Street, presumably for help, and had just reached the doorway. I had no more than a glimpse of what was happening before one of the other uncles closed the door and the emergency phone calls began. Arthur died in hospital, aged only forty-eight. He was our favourite uncle, a warm, buoyant and generous presence in our early lives, associated with imaginative treats, which for me included, during my riding school days, an excursion to some remote cinema—was it the Roxy, Sandringham?—to see *Florian*, a film set in Vienna with one of the famous Lipizzaner stallions as eponymous hero. He would have helped reconnect us with the world, and broken through the reserve which was my mother's way of dealing with her grief. Two years later, his wife Kathleen, whom we also loved greatly, died from heart trouble, leaving an eight-year-old daughter to be brought up by Kathleen's mother and sister. Against this background of seemingly endless loss, I stayed on for a year or more with the other two uncles, but when Jack, the gentle ironist with whom I swapped lines from the Marx Brothers, was diagnosed with cancer, 33 Collins Street became unbearably sad. Soon after Jack's death early in 1954, aged fifty-three, our lawyer uncle Michael departed for Greece as Australian Consul-General. He died in January 1960, a few years after his return, aged fifty-seven. That left the youngest brother, Desmond, bereft, and although I was fond of him we couldn't do much to help one another. The family structure, based on the confidence, resourcefulness and affection of the five closely united Niall brothers, had crumbled to nothing. There was no common medical factor: just bad luck. Only Desmond lived a normal life span.

Santamaria's unexpected offer was welcome. I needed a job and the only ones to come my way so far were not promising. An arts degree wasn't much use, except as a preliminary to teaching or librarianship. One of the graduates from my honours year was proofreading the telephone directory in the hope of somehow moving into publishing, which I think she may have done eventually. On the strength of my mastery of medical terms I applied for the position of librarian at the Eye and Ear Hospital, but didn't get it. The German Consul wanted a secretary. I had scarcely a word of German, and my typing was slow and inaccurate. *Rural Life* sounded more interesting than these so I thought I would give it a try. It was easier than it sounded: a matter of scanning newspapers and Department of Agriculture press releases for good news stories about migration, decentralisation, irrigation, soil reclamation and family life on the land. With summaries of journal articles, reports from the rural groups, and some primitive laying out of the text for the printer, I managed well enough; and during my short tenure as editor I changed the large format newsheet to an octavo-size magazine style with a few gum trees on the cover. It wasn't daring, but it was an improvement. Given a free hand to add anything I pleased within the small page span, I began to write book reviews and feature articles, including one on country kitchens. I might have done more with *Rural Life* or even used that experience as a way into professional journalism, if the scene had not changed so suddenly and dramatically.

In October 1954, after losing the federal election, the ALP leader Dr H.V. [Bert] Evatt made his famous attack on Santamaria's Movement. He accused 'a small minority group of Labor members' of being disloyal to the party and his leadership. Their activities were directed, he said, from outside the Labor movement. Within a few days the *Sydney Morning Herald* identified the 'outside influence' as B.A. Santamaria, and named several Labor members as Santamaria's men. Angry at losing the prime ministership, which had seemed within his grasp, Evatt found, or pretended to find, a cluster of conspiracies, which included Menzies as well as Santamaria. The election followed Menzies' announcement of a royal commission into communist activities in Australia. This followed the defection, in April 1954, of Vladimir Petrov, third secretary to the Russian embassy in Canberra. Communism became an election issue and may well have been decisive in the ALP defeat. Evatt had courted the Catholic vote and even invited Santamaria to help with his policy speech, so his sudden discovery of saboteurs had more than a touch of theatre.[4]

Reading the *Sydney Morning Herald* in Santamaria's office I was almost as surprised as Dr Evatt pretended to be. Having drifted into official Catholic Action[5], I was only just beginning to understand its unofficial side, in the industrial groups whose success in voting communists out of trade unions had given Movement men a large measure of power within the ALP to which the unions were affiliated. No one ever asked me to join anything or to promise secrecy; and for all the melodrama with which the press surrounded Santamaria's office, I found it open, informal, and with no security at all. Anyone would have answered my questions, if I had known there were questions to ask.

My ignorance was partly due to my limited education: no Australian history, no knowledge of Australian politics. I knew about the Movement's wins in the unions but didn't take in the implications of the resultant power in the ALP, nor the complex loyalties involved. At that time Santamaria's office in Swanston Street, Melbourne, was the official headquarters of the National Secretariat of Catholic Action, of which he was the Director. I was working for the Australian bishops—hardly a controversial set of employers, I would then have thought. In fact I didn't give it much thought at all. I was preoccupied with family tragedies in that bleak year.

Once established in the job, I was curiously isolated by the nature of my work. The other women were all secretaries; they took phone calls and typed letters, and presumably were in touch with whatever was happening. Most of them had probably come in through parish groups, and in that way learned the history and structure of the Movement. I scarcely knew our parish priest, and had never joined any group of any kind. I could have learned more in the Newman Society at Melbourne University but the serious talk about religion and politics went on in the pub or in the *Catholic Worker* group, from which women were excluded. Vincent Buckley's study of the current of ideas among Catholics at Melbourne University, in *Cutting Green Hay* (1982) lists all the influential figures of the 1940s and 1950s. Again, no women. In the 1960s, the decade of Germaine Greer, some Catholic women intellectuals emerged, with Joanne

McLean (later Joanne Lee Dow) as a strong presence. None, to my knowledge, in the 1950s, claimed equality in discussion—probably because they were never present to hear it. I had a few friends among the younger men in Buckley's circle but lost touch with them soon after my final year. Apart from one or two Newman Society lectures, I missed the whole experience that Buckley describes. Recently, reading a comprehensive history of the Campion Society, the first and most influential group of Melbourne Catholic intellectuals, I am not surprised by its primary sources: interviews with sixty-seven men and only two women, one of them the widow of a founding member.[6]

In Santamaria's office the divide was the same. None of the women ever went to the weekly meetings at which current happenings and policies were discussed. At lunch time, the men played cricket in the narrow back yard behind the office which, from mid-1955, was a Fitzroy terrace house. Inside, the women sat together and knitted, or went out, as I usually did. With my former school friend Susan Parker, who was also working for the Rural Movement, I sometimes went to the newly established Pellegrini's in Bourke Street for our first delicious experiences of pasta and espresso coffee. But lunch with the men, inside or outside the office, never happened. There was nothing surprising about that. In the 1950s the separation between the men who made decisions and the women who typed and carried tea trays was almost universally observed. Nearly all the secretaries in Santamaria's office lived with their parents, although several were in their thirties. Here or elsewhere in the 1950s, equal pay was rare; and so it was seldom possible for a single woman to have a flat or a house of her own. This should have worried me more than it did.

If I had known more I wouldn't have strolled into the maelstrom of October 1954. Not because I would have thought the Movement wrong or mistaken, but because by temperament I usually took the 'yes, but ...' position. The text 'He that is not with me is against me' made me uneasy. I hated conflict. But there I was, in the middle of one of Australia's biggest political and ideological battles. I had to choose. Because I saw the split, both political and religious, so suddenly and from the perspective of those under attack, my sympathies were engaged. Even though I lacked commitment to the cause, and was already socially isolated, I thought it would be ignoble to resign. Safe on Kew Hill I hadn't known the sectarianism that many other Catholics encountered. Now that I was behind the stockade, I felt a new sense of tribal loyalty.

In the stack of newspapers to which the office subscribed, I read about the sinister arch-plotter whom I couldn't recognise in the easygoing, friendly Santamaria. It was a lesson in point of view. Each side thought of itself as the defender, not the aggressor. There was huge damage, with victims on both sides. The Victorian ALP government was defeated in 1955, and Evatt lost another federal election later in the same year. Most of the 'Movement men' lost their seats. In the main, Santamaria was held accountable. Yet the authority of the Catholic Church had been involved from the beginning. If the Movement was wrong, so were the Bishops; and so was their insistence on a disastrous policy of secrecy, which stemmed from sectarian fears. Santamaria and his wife and family had a hard time; his sudden notoriety and their distinctive surname made invisibility impossible. There was a great deal of bitterness, and I lost some friends. On both sides, tolerance had its limits; there wasn't much that you could call dialogue in those days. The experience gave me a lasting dislike of labelling people, painfully acquired but useful in a biographer.

While pondering this new situation, I responded to the human variety of Santamaria's office. Where else would I meet both a Polish baron and a waterside worker who had been bashed by communist rivals in his union elections? The Marlon Brando film *On the Waterfront* (1954) had just been screened in Melbourne. The story of quietly-spoken Gus Alford, who had 'taken on Big Jim Healy' and won office as secretary of the Waterside Workers Federation, was almost as exciting; and it was real. It gave a human dimension to stories of the ballot rigging, violence and intimidation that preceded the secret ballots legislation of 1949 and 1951.

Baron Adam Gubrynowicz, who had been in charge of protocol in the Foreign Affairs department in prewar Poland, came every morning to read the airmail edition of the London *Times*. A postwar migrant, whose elegant wife worked on the cosmetics counter at George's, Collins

Street, the Baron had a certain threadbare distinction and a highly developed sense of theatre. 'A little against me this morning, I think?' he would say if my good morning greeting seemed offhand. At mid-morning precisely he would announce that it was time to brief Santamaria on the day's doings in Europe, as revealed in the *Times*. 'I go to my audience with our leader', he would say. His style was a consciously ironic parody of past grandeurs in diplomatic circles. Only the buoyant and amusing chaplain, Father Eric D'Arcy (later Archbishop of Tasmania, but then a lecturer in philosophy at Melbourne University) played the Baron's game with the same comic flair.

The refugee and the waterside worker gave windows to other worlds. But if that was an enlargement of experience, it came with an equal constriction. Having grown up in one enclosure, I had settled into another. To venture outside it was to feel the anger and distress of Catholics for whom the split in the Australian Labor Party was a personal and political tragedy. I was now defined by my job; and it was not always an apt or comfortable fit. Invited to Sydney by one of my mother's lifelong friends, I had my first 'don't mention the war' experience. It was very gentle, but it left its impression. High Court judge Sir Edward McTiernan was a kindly host (though inclined to recount the finer points of past judgments) and my sisters and I loved his much younger wife Kathleen. Arriving there for a few days' holiday some time after the Split, I was greeted conspiratorially by Kathleen: 'It upsets Edward so much, it's best not to mention Santamaria'. McTiernan and Evatt were old friends. The loyalty was unassailable, even if Evatt had become, as Kathleen said,'a little erratic'.

On that visit, however, I must have found a quiet corner to mention the war to Sir Edward's temporary associate, Wilfrid Sheed, son of the London and New York publishers Frank Sheed and Maisie Ward. Wilfrid, who had just graduated from Oxford, was using the long stretches of High Court proceedings, when he should have been attending to Sir Edward, to write his first novel *A Middle Class Education.* Amused by my *Rural Life* editorship, he used some more High Court time to write me a witty piece about the boredom of country living, which I published in the next issue. No one seemed to mind; perhaps no one read it. Wilfrid Sheed's certainty about being a novelist was enviable; so was his family publishing house, and his easy knowledge of the international literary scene. That was a world I would have liked to enter.

In the series of explosions that followed the Evatt attack, *Rural Life* vanished, as did the Movement. The National Civic Council emerged, as an organisation of laymen, free of episcopal control. In compensation for the loss of *Rural Life* I was given the Books page of *News Weekly*, which had been the unofficial organ of the Movement. Although its *raison d'être* was political and industrial propaganda, and its tone strident, it gave a good deal of space to reviews of books and films with no particular agenda except to entertain. Large enticing parcels of new books came in every few days. I was pleased to get sole possession of this domain. Sometimes the leading review was written by Santamaria, or some designated person. Sometimes I wrote the whole page myself, with brief reviews of novels and detective stories, and perhaps a biography in the lead. I learned the basic skills of sub-editing and layout from the editor Ted Madden. A film buff who had worked as an extra in *On the Beach,* Ted was always ready for a talk about films, or anything else, on Tuesday afternoons, after the weekly paper had been put to bed. We couldn't pay for reviews, but I occasionally commissioned them, with the book as the only reward. Father John Fahey, a Jesuit with a nice laconic style, could be tempted by some light reading. He used to sign his reviews 'XT'. 'Was that Xavier T?', I asked. No, it meant extra terrible.

The political and religious storms outside were not reflected in the office routine, nor were they talked about among the women. Belatedly, however, I was learning current affairs through my morning task of scanning the Australian newspapers for items of interest which I cut out for Santamaria. Soon I could distinguish between the editorials that said something and those that didn't. I knew all the trade union acronyms, from AFULE to FEDFA and WWF, and could identify at a glance the characteristic layout of every national daily. I always dipped into the *Sydney Morning Herald*'s Saturday pages where in 1956 I read A.D. Hope's funny and outrageous review of Patrick White's *The Tree of Man*. Each morning, while I worked through fifteen Australian dailies (with a double ration on Mondays) the Baron, on the other side of a glass partition, read *The Times*. Weeklies and quarterlies by the dozen, like the *Economist* and the *Far Eastern Economic Review*, went to Santamaria, who must have spent hours on them every evening.

Always a quick reader, I had no trouble getting through the newspapers, discarding repetition and looking out for anything interesting under the general headings of religion, politics, economics and social and industrial affairs. Filing the cuttings for future reference wasn't so easy. My improvised system didn't leave nearly enough space for expansion. *Après moi le déluge,* I thought, cramming stout folders into overcrowded filing cabinets. It couldn't go on forever. But still I didn't plan or even imagine a future for myself.

My social life had virtually stopped with the end of university life; and unless I changed jobs it wasn't likely to improve. Family life, always varied and entertaining, filled the gap. I was proud of my younger brother and sisters, growing up to be more venturesome than I had been, and beginning to leave home. Hugh, who won first place in Victoria in his Matriculation exams in 1954, went into college. Margaret battled the Genazzano obstacle course in physics and chemistry to do a degree in science. Frances, the youngest, would later choose to change schools and board at Loreto, Mary's Mount, in Ballarat. There were two enchanting babies of the next generation, and more to come with the marriages of all my siblings. I liked being an aunt but was uneasy about the dependent daughter-at-home role that could have claimed me permanently.

Marriage seemed both elusive and inevitable. Late in 1956, taking my lunch hour in the city, I met a friend from university days who invited me to dinner. We began to see each other quite often and soon we were engaged. On both sides it was an impetuous decision but it seemed so suitable that no one could have called it reckless. A lawyer with a brilliant academic record, Jesuit-educated at Xavier and Newman colleges, he was good-looking and agreeable. For him, marriage was premature because he wanted to practise as a barrister. This would mean an uncertain income for some years. I am shocked now to remember that it never occurred to me to work after marriage. I have to remind myself that this was normal thinking at a time when women teachers and public servants had to resign when they married. There was a certain social stigma too for a family with a working wife. In my schooldays the phrase 'her mother works' was whispered in a tone of condolence: clearly something was amiss in *that* household. I would have been happy to leave the workforce and be like everyone else. Yet as the rituals of the announcement, the ring, the exchange of family visits took over, I felt uncertain. Were we really right for one another? Was I just trying to get back the life represented by Kew Hill? I was good at communicating doubt, and soon I had both of us worried. Embarrassed and self-reproachful, I broke the engagement.

With my wedding plans cancelled, my mother suggested an overseas holiday. She thought of it as a compensation for having kept me from Oxford, for which she always felt guilty. I had a happy irresponsible time, travelling in congenial company with schoolfriend Mary Donohoe and staying with friends and relatives in Britain and the United States. I met my new sister-in-law Ann Morgan who had married my brother John in London in the previous year. They were living in Boston, where John was continuing his postgraduate work in medicine. Ann who had spent the 1950s in specialist medical training, was astonished at my lack of ambition and alarmed at my representation of women's lives in the Melbourne she was soon to enter. For her there was no contradiction between motherhood and a medical career, and she was to prove it, with great distinction, in years to come. Her influence on our family was to be profound, but she was tactful and took time to let us feel it.

Home in Melbourne, still unfocused, I took on the Mannix biography as a short-term project too interesting to refuse. I told my doubting self that I would either marry or look for a job in publishing; this would not be forever. But short term it was not: it was a huge assignment. The interviews came first but there were large topics to explore. One was the question of Catholic education and state aid: how did that look in 1913, when Mannix arrived in Melbourne? I spent weeks in trawling through bound volumes of a defunct periodical *Austral Light* at the Central Catholic Library, or past issues of the

Catholic Weekly and the *Advocate*. The Director of the Catholic Library, Father Phillips, was polite but sceptical, as well he might have been. So was Father Stormon, who showed me the Hibernica collection in the Newman College Library. Both men were scholars who knew what a Mannix biography should involve, and in those patriarchal times they would not have thought much of a young woman's chances of understanding the great man's career. They did not offer advice, but let me go on making notes, on conscription, on the Irish question, on the building of Newman College. It was an interesting, if wasteful, exercise in self-education. Probably some of it was useful but as I typed my notes in Santamaria's Fitzroy office I could not be sure.

When I had more or less given up on the Mannix project I visited the eighty-year-old parish priest at Oakleigh, Father Coyne, an Irishman who had been a seminarian at Maynooth. By chance, quite recently, I discovered one typed page from this meeting, misplaced among some old letters of my own, and probably never given to Santamaria. It makes me feel better about my interviewing skills. I was not the only one to be defeated by the Archbishop's silence.

Fr Coyne.

A student for 5 years of Dr Mannix's presidency. The students of that time knew D.M. as aloof and very severe. 'We loved him not—not at all.' He exerted what seemed unnecessarily strict discipline. If any of the students wanted to go into Dublin, to the dentist, the oculist, etc, he had to write to his own Bishop for permission, and that permission might be some time in coming. The College dentist came once a week.

Life at Maynooth was a hard one—no luxuries or distractions. Students seldom felt that they had enough to eat—one good meal a day and two very light meals supplemented by bread and butter. President not blamed for this—funds were scarce … We loved him not—but he was a great man.

[BN: 'But he was loved later, in Australia?']

'Yes, but that was after he had been attacked, insulted, misrepresented, over conscription, the Irish question … the people reacted against the treatment he got.'

'He wasn't a man you could know. No one knew him, not even Jerry Murphy.'

[BN: 'Father Hackett?']

'No, but they knew him as well as anyone. There was always a wall. You could go so far, and then you might ask a question—you wouldn't get an answer—. He used to sing, sometimes, for Father Moynihan. Father Moynihan could get him to sing—but there was always a wall.'

[BN: What would happen if you asked a question that he thought intrusive?]

'Nothing. But you wouldn't get an answer. He would ignore it.'

He never wrote his speeches. Just a few notes on the back of an envelope usually. The speech for the Irish Race Convention was one of the few he prepared in

> *detail. He wrote many letters—his housekeeper used to say he could write a hundred in a night—he would address them and drop them on the floor.*

It was painful to think of all those letters, and about Monsignor Fox's exasperating box of Christmas cards. I wish I had asked Father Coyne about the singing. Did the Archbishop sing Irish ballads? Was music important to him? And what was the magical power of persuasion held by Father Moynihan? The two Irish Jesuits, Jeremiah Murphy, Rector of Newman College, and William Hackett, Director of the Central Catholic Library, had died in the mid-1950s. Was it for their wit and ebullience that Mannix valued them? Did he need such buoyant spirits around him? With such questions unanswered, Mannix remained forever behind that wall. Much later, when I read Vincent Buckley's *Cutting Green Hay* I recognised the qualities that had charmed and baffled me. Buckley recalled the distinctive quality of Mannix's humour: '[It was] a humour gentle, courteous, beautifully timed, based on an intense awareness of *vanitas vanitatum* in which an unillusioned mockery of the world's ways coiled back in a self mockery that added to rather than threatened his authority. It was a technique of the multiple double-take.'[7]

Buckley tempered strong disapproval of the Movement with admiration for Santamaria's engaging humour, his 'existential courage and a great charm based on courtesy'. Pondering the choice of the very young

Santamaria for a major role in the Australian Catholic Church, he concluded that Mannix responded most to men of energy and vision who followed their own initiatives. Hence his liking for Murphy and Hackett, 'both very witty, rather eccentric individualists with a zany touch of humour', who were also very capable administrators on their own territory. Santamaria, in Buckley's view, was 'an exhilarating paradox'. As a functionary of Mannix and the church, Buckley said, he was the very opposite of all that functionary means: he was informal, inventive, wide-ranging, adaptable.

If Buckley's essays on Mannix and Santamaria had been available at the time of my interviews, they would have helped me to understand why the Mannix biography was so intractable. It might have led to the Murphy and Hackett papers that I never thought to explore. One problem, which I did understand, was that Santamaria was too close to his subject. He could not extol Mannix's wisdom in matters of church and state without sounding self-congratulatory about his own role; and he was wary of that. He did not like to talk about his own feelings. Eloquent on most topics, he became embarrassed and inarticulate in talking about his wife and children, whom he loved deeply. His style and that of his family was one of self-deprecating irony. This was very engaging but it did not help him in writing about Mannix. Once, he asked me in some distress to search the Sydney papers for a report of a speech in which he had referred to 'the Archbishop whom I love more than my own father'.

He was appalled at having made this uncharacteristic slip; and dreaded its becoming known to the older Santamaria. It probably never did. But it alerted me to the immense and unacknowledgeable gulf between the old patrician at Raheen and the Italian migrant father in his Brunswick greengrocer's shop. To be a loving son to both, as Santamaria was, cannot have been easy.

The Santamaria biography could not fully engage with the complex loyalties and prejudices of the time. Older Australian Catholics of Irish background, like Evatt's deputy Arthur Calwell, were possessive about 'their' Archbishop. Santamaria's status as an outsider of Italian parentage reinforced the widespread feeling that he was too clever, too quick, too enterprising. An invader in an Irish-Australian church, he had no business interfering in the Labor movement. Yet Mannix had chosen him, and few wanted to blame the tribal leader. The Catholic intellectuals who were the Movement's most articulate critics knew that they owed a great deal to the education system that Mannix had built and to the liberal spirit which did not stifle their opposition to the policies of his later years. Revering Mannix while deploring Santamaria was inconsistent but understandable. In the wider community, multiculturalism was a long way off. A pamphlet titled 'The Black Hand of Santamaria' aroused a predictable shudder. 'The Black Hand of Murphy'? Not quite the same.

I was not, however, so much concerned with Santamaria's problems as with my own. I became almost sure that he would never write the biography and it was more than time for me to do something on my own account. The obvious course was to go back to my interrupted postgraduate work, but Melbourne University held too many memories of my unhappy finals year. Luckily, a chance meeting with poet and academic Philip Martin solved the problem. I hadn't seen Philip since our student days, but as we stepped aside from the lunchtime city crowd to talk I found it surprisingly easy to explain my predicament. Always in a hurry, yet with endless leisure for friends, Philip listened and offered a solution.

He was moving to the Australian National University as a lecturer in Alec Hope's small but lively English Department: why didn't I enrol there? Next day he telephoned Hope, who was delighted to have me, and within a few weeks I was in Canberra arranging my enrolment. Australia's most distinguished poet and a hard-working academic, Alec Hope seemed to have all the time in the world for a stroll across the paddocks to show me over the makeshift library of those early ANU days. Hope offered me a postgraduate scholarship, which I had the satisfaction of refusing. In that way my guilt about wasting the award from Melbourne was expunged. Not that it cost me much: my mother, always generous, was subsidising me, even though she would have liked me to stay at home. But I wasn't needed there; family life had renewed itself. My mother, who had been over-anxious with her own children, especially in her first years as a widow, was a relaxed, loving and tolerant grandmother. She found creative pleasure in restoring and redecorating a series of houses that she bought and resold. I doubt if she made much money for her work, but her artistic and managerial gifts were given expression.

My time in Canberra was happy and sociable. I made good some of the reading I'd neglected in my time at Melbourne University, went to poetry readings, sat in on Manning Clark's quirky Australian History lectures. I did coursework in American Literature with the fourth-year honours students, sat for the exams, and got first-class honours: a good omen for my thesis on Edith Wharton which later had the same success. The Wharton thesis, supervised by informal and amusing Bob Brissenden, was a good choice, well ahead of the rediscovery of her novels in the mid-1960s by the women's movement. My only problem was the long delays in getting copies of her works from secondhand bookshops in New York. Except for *The Age of Innocence* and *The House of Mirth*, Wharton's novels and other writings were out of print, and even interlibrary loans didn't produce a full set. In one way this was good news: it suggested that I was working in a more or less untilled field. But I was impatient to get on with it, sure I had something to say. At Melbourne, in my previous attempt at postgraduate work, I had taken notes on the poorly chosen topic of T.S. Eliot's ventures into poetic drama but hadn't written a word. Now I was writing easily and with pleasure: the chapters seemed to shape themselves. Was it Wharton's fiction, with its witty, poignant exploration of women's lives in a remote yet recognisable past, that made the difference, or the new sense of freedom that came with the move to Canberra? It was probably both.

Canberra in the early 1960s was still in the making, semi-rural. Today's imposing public buildings—the National Library, the High Court, the National Gallery—were yet to come. There was no lake. With just two cinemas, one at Civic, the other at Manuka, and no professional theatre, there wasn't much choice of entertainment. The ANU's School of General Studies, which until 1957 had been Canberra University College, had few postgraduate students. That suited me; it was easier to make friends in a place that was still evolving, its doors wide open to newcomers. In fact most people were newcomers; someone born in the fledgeling national capital was a rarity. I spent my first month or two, late in 1962, in University House, which was elegantly designed, comfortable, and in those early years still within the means of postgraduates. I really wanted a flat, but because of Canberra's acute housing shortage, in which people often paid exorbitant sums in key money, it was a hopeless quest. Here, as in my well-timed meeting with Philip Martin, I was lucky. Another friend from Melbourne University, Bob Beveridge, whom I hadn't seen since his departure for Oxford in 1953, offered to sublet his flat to me while he went on a year's study leave. After a short wait, during which I spent Christmas in Melbourne, I moved into this first home of my own, fully furnished, and equipped with a beautiful architect's work-table which doubled as a dining table. There I gave my first dinner parties, using the cookbook Bob's mother had given him, to which she had added such basic directions as TURN ON OVEN.

I have only one bad memory from an exceptionally happy year. Somewhere, I think at a lecture by some visiting scholar, I met a senior diplomat, a Melbourne man, a Catholic with ALP affiliations, who recognised my name and remembered my father. I must come to lunch, he said; he and his wife would look after me, introduce me to some people in Foreign Affairs, make sure I saw more of Canberra than the university. That sounded promising, and I duly went to Sunday lunch where all was smiles and friendliness until I was asked what I'd done before coming to ANU, and the name Santamaria rattled the coffee spoons. My host became glacial, and then extremely rude. His wife was embarrassed. I finished my coffee and left, reflecting afterwards that if Bob Santamaria had inadvertently asked a communist or former communist to lunch he wouldn't have forgotten a host's duty of courtesy. I resented being judged on my presumed opinions, which were in fact not at all easily defined. To harangue a young woman, an invited guest in his own house, was unbecoming behaviour and I wondered how the diplomat managed his anger in professional situations. I wrote a chilly note of thanks to his wife, in the hope that its formal correctness would make them both feel uncomfortable. I never saw either of them again. The experience confirmed my sense that in many quarters, and perhaps most of all among Catholics, dialogue about the Movement was impossible. When I was ready to sort out my political and religious beliefs I would do it quietly, on my own.

In many ways I would have liked to stay in Canberra and convert my MA thesis to a PhD. But I needed to earn my living, and to give back Bob Beveridge's flat, so with the thesis still unfinished I wrote three job applications. Timing for an academic career was perfect as the new universities that opened in the early 1960s were looking for staff. I applied to Melbourne, Monash and ANU. Three interviews brought offers from the heads of all three English Departments: Ian Maxwell, Bill Scott and Alec Hope. My lack of teaching experience might have counted against me; so might my having worked with Mannix and Santamaria. Alec Hope showed a mild interest in those controversial names on my scanty *cv*. The others ignored them. 'Referees?' Bill Scott asked, only to brush aside his own question. 'We can be your referees, can't we, Tom?' he said, turning to his fellow interviewer and senior colleague, Tom Dobson, who remembered me from Old English classes at Melbourne. I could hardly believe my luck in being able to start all over again in a new world. I didn't seriously consider the Melbourne offer, though it was a satisfaction to be given it. Hesitating between the other two, I chose Monash, because it was new, and because it was being shaped by Bill Scott whom I judged, rightly, to be kind and shrewd. Although dropping my thesis at Melbourne, breaking my engagement, and abandoning the Mannix biography might have looked like a habit of retreat, I knew that this time I had got it right.

I had a few moments of regret in November 1963 when Archbishop Mannix died, at the age of ninety-nine. Although I had disappointed Santamaria by giving up on his project, I kept my friendship with him and his family; and I was proved right in my sense that he was not ready for the biography. He must have put it aside for many years. It was published in 1984, twenty-five years after I first interviewed Dr Mannix. I was right too in thinking that the private self of the Archbishop would scarcely appear. Santamaria's *Daniel Mannix* is an intelligent and interesting study of the public man but at the personal level it is, inevitably, idealised. A study of unfailing courage and high achievement, it doesn't show a private self with the sadness, the regrets, the doubts, that even a great man—perhaps especially a great man—must experience. But it was not my book and never could have been. My time in Canberra opened up all kinds of possibilities. I wasn't yet ready to be a writer; I was unsure of myself as an academic, but I had my first taste of independence. More than once, as I walked home on Ainslie Avenue to the nondescript seven-storey Braddon Flats, I thought with great satisfaction: 'No one knows where I am at this moment, and no one knows who I am'.

4

New Haven Winter

Latecomers can be lucky, as I was in the accidental timing of my start in an academic career in the early 1960s when the Australian university system was suddenly expanding. No longer was there just a single establishment in each capital city. Monash and La Trobe in Victoria, Macquarie in New South Wales and Flinders in South Australia were all 1960s foundations. There were new ideas for courses, ample staffing and a spirit of optimism. Monash was not literally red brick (it was oddly multicoloured with purplish-brown, grey or pinkish-yellow brick buildings) but it made a functional response to the grey stone cloisters and clock towers that were every Australian's idea of a university. Arts and economics and politics faculties were housed in the eleven-storey Menzies Building which had the novelty of two lifts, reserved for staff, and an escalator for the students. These divisions soon lapsed, not just because students began to contest them, but because staff members found the escalators quicker. The flat outer suburban setting was as charmless as the huge car park. But it was the future (or we thought it was) and it was exhilarating to be making something new.

I started my Monash career in January 1964 as a teaching fellow (or tutor) in a small room, with new and very basic furniture which reflected the optimism of the time about teaching patterns as well as my status on the academic ladder. Taking the measure of my domain in the weeks before term began, I looked nervously at the stack of ten chairs for students, not realising what a luxury it was to have tutorial groups limited to such a small number. With academic hierarchies in mind the architects had designed rooms accordingly. Professors had four windows from which to survey the car park or the muddy stretches which would one day be lawns; they had three walls of bookshelving, a couch, two or three armchairs and several filing cabinets. I was very happy with my two windows and the nameplate on the door which proved my new existence. Uncertain about nearly everything else, I knew exactly how to arrange the three drawers of the dark green filing cabinet. Poetry in the top drawer, Fiction in the middle and Drama at the bottom. These reflected the three terms of the academic year, and the familiar order of teaching. Later I would have a bigger room, three windows and several filing cabinets but it would be many years before biography and autobiography demanded spaces of their own. Although Monash, like ANU, was less reverently disposed than Melbourne to F.R. Leavis's Great Tradition of literature, more pluralist, willing to look at Australian and American writing which the older universities hadn't yet noticed, it still based its teaching on the three literary genres.

In my first half-dozen years as an academic, pleasure came well before ambition. In fact, ambition was scarcely needed, because promotion came easily. I enjoyed tutorials, seminars and thesis supervision; and an indulgent head of department spared me the ordeal of the lecture theatre. 'Plenty of the others like the sound of their own voices', Bill Scott said when I queried his promoting me to a lectureship. I would have regretted it later, but at that stage I was contented with my first promotion, to the senior tutorship which followed my ANU thesis result. This was a tenured but non-career position at which several women in other Arts departments were indefinitely halted. Instead, Bill Scott recommended the next promotion without even asking me to give lecturing a try. He sympathised with my fear of public speaking and played down its importance. It was not just indulgence on his part. He valued small group teaching, the pastoral care of students, whether gifted or struggling, and thesis supervision, all areas in which I became confident. Bill Scott was often described as a brilliant administrator, a term which doesn't convey his instinct for listening and responding to individual needs and abilities, building on strengths. Orchestration might be a better word. Settling in as a lecturer who by tacit agreement never lectured (or hardly ever, even in later years) I couldn't have asked for anything better than the intellectual stimulus, companionship and fun of the Monash English Department in the expansive 1960s. Nor could anyone have been happier than I was to be able to buy my own house: even to have my own mortgage was a pleasure.

In and out of class in those early, well-staffed Monash years, students were central. We all had time to read the first poems or plays they brought in for an opinion. The English Department was full of gifted, hard-working, friendly and amusing colleagues; and I never cease to wonder at my luck and good sense in choosing Monash against the job offers from Melbourne and ANU. Determined not to create a clone or colony of Melbourne University, Bill Scott chose staff from states other than Victoria and from Britain. Geoffrey Hiller was from Tasmania, Francis King from Perth; both came to Monash after Cambridge, as did Queensland graduate Harold Love. Elaine Barry, also from Queensland, had studied in South Carolina. Very few Melbourne graduates were appointed, and none came without experience of other places. Bruce Steele had been at Durham University, Jenny Strauss at New England, and Philip Martin, like me, came by way of ANU. Directly from Britain came such outstanding scholars—and quirky personalities—as Frank Wilson whose field was Yeats; and Peter Sucksmith, a distinguished Dickens scholar whose sense of theatre, in timing and the outrageously deployed strategy of tears, had the true Dickensian spirit

In scholarly achievement and cultural creativity the English Department was productive, but without pressure to orthodoxy. Peter Sucksmith's *The Narrative Art of Charles Dickens*, Douglas Muecke's *The Compass of Irony*, and Dennis Bartholomeusz' *Macbeth and the Players* were published in London in the late 1960s; and there were many more to come, not least the prodigious and varied scholarly work of Harold Love. In the 1960s and early 1970s Philip Martin and Jenny Strauss were publishing their poems and giving readings on campus. English department members were central to staff–student theatre of the time. Their productions ranged from the highly professional to under-rehearsed entertainments that released the ham actor within some unlikely academics. One of the most professional productions was Elaine Barry's *Playboy of the Western World*, with Max Gillies, one of Monash's first honours graduates, brilliant in the lead role. Patricia O'Sullivan was a strong, beautiful Pegeen and Harold Love, cast against type, played an irascible Old Mahon. Dennis Bartholomeusz gave a remarkable Shakespeare course in which an annual production developed his students' skills in stage and costume design, lighting and music, as well as acting. Richard Pannell played a memorable Gloucester to Dennis Pryor's Lear, in a production by Elaine Barry and Dennis Bartholomeusz. Dennis Davison's fruity melodramas, in which nearly everything went wrong on the night, brought the diffident and untalented, staff as well as students, to try their skills, urged on by Dennis's unquenchable good humour. There was for many years no music department in the university, and in its absence English staff members Bruce Steele (an accomplished musician who was also the university organist), Francis King and Harold Love, with Bruce Knox from History, helped to fill the gap with a weekly program of public recitals. Patrick McCaughey's Visual Arts department and gallery was still to come.

Alec King, appointed to the second chair in 1965, was English, and had taught in the University of Western Australia, as had the next professorial appointment, David Bradley, a graduate of Melbourne University and Cambridge. Both Alec and David, in their different styles, were exceptional teachers, remembered for giving a strong sense of what literature meant to them and could mean to their students. With a first year enrolment of six hundred students, lectures had to be divided into four sessions on the same day, two each taken by the same lecturers. The big audiences demanded a sense of theatre. Author and editor Peter Rose, a first year student in 1973, was at David Bradley's opening lecture of that year, which he recalls as 'magnificent' in voice, movement and presence: 'His reading of *The Windhover* I can still hear—a great experience'.[1]

Remembering that range of talent, it seems to me that in my first few years at Monash I made up for my very patchy education at Melbourne. I must have read some of the Romantic poets, at least enough for a finals paper in the period, but I owe the real discovery of Wordsworth to Francis King, and that of Keats to Peter Naish. Later we were too busy for the luxury of going to one another's lectures, but in the early 1960s I made many discoveries—not least in teaching which I enjoyed well beyond my cautious expectations.

It took time for Monash to compete in public esteem with the older university in Carlton; and though its staff members knew their own abilities, it was another matter to get through to competitive teachers and status-conscious parents. An anecdote of the early years: one mother to another. 'How did your daughter get on in the Matric exams?' 'She's got a place at Monash.' 'Oh dear, I *am* sorry.' Knowing our secondary status and sometimes irritated by it, we probably became a more cohesive group than most university departments. Geographical isolation was important. Outer suburban Monash had no diversions to compare with Melbourne University's Carlton environs. We had no cafés, restaurants or cinemas, and only one rather dreary staff club. Thrown on our own resources for companionship and entertainment, we formed friendships which are still strong today. Many were in their first jobs; some were far from home. Because so many were new to Melbourne, we became to a large extent one another's family. Over thirty years or more we went through the cycles of life together: love, marriages, babies, the deaths of parents, the good and bad times alike. There were house-moving days and painting and carpentry work sessions, as well as dinner parties, welcomes and farewells. If you wanted a garden shed demolished or a tree lopped, you need look no further for help than your multi-skilled colleagues. After Bill Scott became Deputy Vice-Chancellor his successors David Bradley, Alec King and Clive Probyn gave strong intellectual leadership with the same attention to the personal element, though under more difficult conditions, as funding and staffing declined in later years.

When it was time for my first overseas study leave in 1967, I chose the United States rather than Oxford or Cambridge. That wasn't a rejection of the dreaming spires. It followed my seemingly haphazard thesis choice at ANU. Having written on the novels of Edith Wharton didn't make me an Americanist, but it was a start. American Literature, one of the specialist areas then being developed at Monash, was flourishing under the direction of Elaine Barry. Student demand was brisk; there was room for a second Americanist. My course work in American Literature at ANU was no substitute for studying in the United States and getting to know the country as well as the university system.

Having won a Fulbright postgraduate award, I spent the academic year 1967–68 in the Middle West, at the University of Michigan, Ann Arbor. Chosen partly for its academic standing but also because it sounded reassuringly small, it was not far from the Canadian border and from Windsor, Ontario, where my sister Margaret was then living with her husband, American academic Gene Le Mire, and their two small children. My neat little apartment on East Washington Street would have been lonely, especially as winter closed in, except for frequent weekends away. The family was nicely placed for me that year, with my brother Hugh (then a research fellow at the National Institute of Health) and his wife Maggie in Virginia and my Gorman cousins, John and Jeanne, in New York. Ann Arbor had the small town feeling of 1960s Canberra—with snow and squirrels instead of sun and swooping magpies—but the university itself, which virtually occupied the whole town, was huge, with no perceptible centre. Compulsory Freshman English for all faculties meant a vast, bureaucratic Department of English, unlike any in Australia. At ANU I'd been one of very few postgraduates, all of us welcomed as members of the department. Michigan had scores of them on the outer fringes, trying to be noticed.

Because of its name Ann Arbor sounded pastoral and placid but this was not a peaceful year. It was a year of civil rights demonstrations, race riots and assassinations, the year in which Martin Luther King and Bobby Kennedy were shot. Too close for comfort to the barricaded streets of Detroit, shoppers in Ann Arbor would flinch at the sound of a car backfiring. Student politics was passionately engaged in civil rights and anti-Vietnam protests. I heard novelist Ralph Ellison speak in a vast crowded auditorium of white students about what it meant to be a black American writer. Accused at question time of not being sufficiently active in the political movement, Ellison replied icily that he was quite angry enough, and 'enlisted for the duration'. The struggle for change was indivisible, he said; white as well as black Americans must be equally committed. Meetings like this gave an added dimension to my reading in black literature—Ellison, Richard Wright and James Baldwin, among many others. A bus ride to Detroit, when even the choice of a seat next to a black passenger meant an awkwardly self-conscious affirmation, mirrored the situation in one of Flannery O'Connor's incisive short stories.

In this atmosphere I was as much engaged in looking around as in studying. I was absorbing the language and customs of the time. The sit-ins, the student power and anti-Vietnam protests which had not yet reached their height at Monash, were daily events at Michigan in 1967. Flower power was fading in a more militant atmosphere, black was beautiful, negro was no longer the polite form. My letters from Michigan expressed culture shock, but by the time I got home in late 1968, it was all happening there too. As in politics, so in religious practice: the times were changing. Michigan's Catholic chaplaincy, quick to move on the liturgical reforms of Vatican Two, invited students to the 'love feast' of the Eucharist. Still nostalgic for the Latin Mass, I wished that whoever was producing the new vernacular forms had a better ear for language. 'Say hello to who you know and who you don't', followed by the handshake or the kiss of peace, might be better than the muttered 'pax vobiscum', but it took some adjustment. As I typed my term papers (unlike their Australian counterparts, every student could type) the study of seventeenth-century New England poetry or the Transcendental movement had strong competition from everyday life in Ann Arbor.

I never quite understood the working of the Michigan Department of English. Compared with any Australian university department it was very formal, headed by famous people who seemed always to be somewhere else, and propped up by an army of lowly teaching assistants, known as graders, who supported themselves through the PhD years by marking students' papers. One of the senior academics, critic and novelist John Aldridge, once asked me if I was meeting other staff members. Hopeful that he was about to offer introductions, I said, 'Well, I don't know many, yet'. 'Neither do I', said Aldridge glumly. Being some years older than most of the postgraduates I didn't quite fit in with them, but they were friendly and sociable. Forever fretting about their chances of employment, they could not believe that I already had a secure position. Life among the graders and the foreign students was probably more fun than among their seniors but I would have liked to see the inner or upper circle.

Lost somewhere in two crowded semesters at Ann Arbor was an idea of reworking my ANU thesis on Edith Wharton. There was too much else to think about, too many new writers to discover. The senior academic staff remained inaccessible. As one of many foreign postgraduate students I wasn't seen as needing attention, and didn't know how to claim it. The American postgraduate students were much more confident and articulate than their Australian counterparts. I watched in wonder at their way of asserting their presence in large seminar groups. The Wharton thesis went home in my baggage, untouched during the Ann Arbor year, and half forgotten. Later I wrote two articles from it, which were published in Australian journals, and left it at that. To do any more I would have needed another stint in the United States, and although the year at Michigan had many rewards I wasn't at all sure that I wanted to try again.

Some years later I had another chance. A famous American scholar, Norman Holmes Pearson, visited Monash. Having heard that I had been at Michigan, he wanted to know what I thought of the American experience. He was interested in Edith Wharton's work which he knew well. I had been discouraged by the fact that her papers, which were held at Yale, were still under embargo while an authorised biography was being written. No difficulty there, Pearson said. The biographer, R.W.B. Lewis, was one of his closest friends. His book, which Pearson was then reading in draft, would soon be published. 'We must get you to Yale', he added, sounding as if he meant it. And he did. It took time to arrange; but everything eventually fell into place before my next leave was due in 1975. Pearson sent a formal offer of a Visiting Fellowship, a promise of access to the Wharton papers, an invitation to join the Yale Americanists at a conference in Texas, and a warm welcome to his department.

With this impressive backing I won a senior scholar's award from the American Council of Learned Societies. These were well-funded, short-term awards, paid in US dollars. A new world of opportunity seemed suddenly to open up for me at one of the famous Ivy League universities. Surprisingly little had as yet been published on Wharton, and no one had gazumped my thesis, even though I had put it aside for so long.

Norman Holmes Pearson was a powerful figure at Yale and in the wider literary world. Everyone knew his name, if only as the co-editor with W.H. Auden of the five-volume anthology of English and American poetry known as 'Auden and Pearson'. He was literary executor for the poet HD (Hilda Doolittle); Robert Penn Warren was one of his friends; he had known Ezra Pound and Robert Frost—indeed just about any literary figure you could mention. During the Second World War Pearson was recruited from Yale by the OSS (Office of Strategic Studies) to head its London desk. His skill in the close reading of literary texts was so useful in assessing documents of doubtful authenticity that he rapidly became a key figure in Allied military intelligence. After the war he put his energies into American cultural programs at home and abroad, while keeping his post at Yale. A large private fortune, said to be inherited from his family's ownership of a Boston department store, gave him independence. His Yale salary paid for his postage stamps, so a colleague said. His collection of paintings by writers ('art for the wrong reasons' as he called it) included one by

Queen Victoria, who qualified because of her diary, and two Lawrences—one by D.H. and the other by his wife Frieda. A New Englander, an authority on Hawthorne with a New England conscience, he was committed to giving international scholars at Yale a sense of the best in the American tradition. A few years before me, Melbourne poet and academic Chris Wallace-Crabbe was welcomed by Norman who became his mentor and introduced him to 'absolutely everybody'. The big names at Yale included Maynard Mack, Richard Ellmann, Harold Bloom, John Hollander, Donald Gallup. It was a dazzling who's who of literary scholars; and during the wakeful hours on the New York flight I felt the excitement of entering the great world.

Before taking the train to New Haven I had a free day in New York. Exhilarated at just being there, enjoying the late autumn sunshine over coffee at a sidewalk café, I felt independent, confident and very pleased with myself for having made it at last to the international scene. After a morning at the Museum of Modern Art, I went to Saks of Fifth Avenue to buy something summery for the Texas conference. Checking designer labels and discreetly written price tags, I thought, why not? This was surely the high point of my career, and should be celebrated. So, after an hour's happy explorations, I found a Dianne Von Fuerstenberg dress which had the virtue of not looking as expensive as it was. Later, with the elegant Saks carrier bag on my arm, I kept a late afternoon appointment at the office of the American Council of Learned Societies, where I was to be welcomed and given my cheque. I was met with grave faces and bad news. Norman Holmes Pearson was very ill; there was great concern about his condition. His secretary had telephoned to say that she would be at the station next day to meet me; and in the meantime I was not to worry too much.

The news hit harder because of the euphoric mood of my day in New York. True to training and habit, I took it calmly, expressed concern, said I would be fine at New Haven; things would work out. It was Norman's tragedy, not mine. I had to hold in my own disappointment, and the sense of a sudden drop in confidence. Recalling it now, I think of it as another 'angel's wings' moment, with the extravagance at Saks of Fifth Avenue an equivalent of my anticipated stage glory as a seven-year-old, and the whisking away of my splendid wings.

Next day I was met at the New Haven railway station by Norman's secretary, who looked distraught. Norman had died the night before, after a short illness, at the age of seventy. With a thousand things to think about, she did well to break the news and install me in the hotel she had booked. A whole empire had collapsed, and there was no one to take on its responsibilities. I was probably not the only visitor to be stranded, but surely my timing could not have been worse. I hadn't known Norman well, but I'd been charmed by his letters, and the thoughtful details of the structured visit he had planned.

A week later there was an impressive memorial service at the University Chapel, at which the Yale chaplain,

William Sloan Coffin, presided. A former student, Tom Wolfe (author of *Radical Chic* and *The Bonfire of the Vanities*), gave a eulogy, with affectionate and amusing anecdotes about Norman's graduate seminars. The head of the English Department, Louis Martz, who had lost a friend of thirty-five years and was desolate, spoke with evident difficulty. Norman's wife was helped to her car, not well enough to speak to anyone. I spent a sad, quiet weekend, assimilating the shock, mourning the lost friendship, and reducing my expectations.

More time for the Wharton papers: it would not be so bad. Nor was it, but what followed was the most solitary period of my life. It was less than eight weeks but seemed much longer. The Texas conference was forgotten. I didn't know anyone in New Haven, and apart from a few seminars in the English Department, and lunch with the two or three academics I eventually located, I spent a six-day week in the Beinecke Manuscripts and Rare Books Library. It was a new experience to feel the serenity of this modern building. Built in granite, translucent marble, bronze and glass, its reading room looks on to a sunken sculpture garden. There is nothing to distract the eyes or break the silence. Perfect if there had been company at lunchtime—but there wasn't.

It was late autumn and the days were very short. The hotel staff warned me not to cross the campus alone after dark: several women had been mugged and one was raped. That made it hard, if not impossible, to go to any of the evening lectures by visiting celebrities.

I always went back to my hotel before the light faded. Before and after dinner in the hotel dining room, where I soon knew the menu by heart, I read or watched old Hitchcock movies in my room. Perhaps in the confusion that followed Pearson's death I was mistaken for a visiting Vice-Chancellor, but I didn't complain about my astonishingly luxurious accommodation at a generous academic discount rate. I was given high-level comfort in the twenty-four storey Sheraton Park Plaza, where I had a big room, with a view of New England spires, trees still in their bright russet colours and a distant prospect of the College Green. Here I read R.W.B. Lewis's *Edith Wharton*. It had been acclaimed, as biographies still were in the 1970s, as the definitive life. With so much time on my hands and the Wharton papers occupying my days, I read more closely and critically than I would otherwise have done. Having spent the day with some of the documents Lewis had used, I began a silent argument with him, thinking, yes, but hadn't he missed something in this incident? Why didn't he do more with that idea? Or, I would read that letter differently.

Although I didn't fully understand it at the time, those weeks on the Wharton papers were a revelation. They showed me the pleasures of using primary sources. They also showed me that there was no such thing as a definitive biography. Lewis's book was a fine piece of scholarly work, well written and psychologically acute. In other circumstances I would probably have thought 'that's that, the Life has been written'. But I was becoming fascinated by the Wharton papers and enjoying the feeling of being almost an insider. The collection was still closed except to scholars with special permission, but Norman Holmes Pearson had arranged that I should see everything. A friendly letter from Lewis, then on leave in Italy, was my passport to the collection.

Re-reading some letters home, I find that the weeks at Yale were not entirely spent in solitary communion with the spirit of Edith Wharton. True, the English Department was elusive, its famous scholars scattered in various parts of the campus, or travelling in Europe. Norman's secretary, whom I visited once or twice, was packing his books and papers; such appointments as hers were personal and soon she would be out of a job. By comparison, Australian university departments were collegial, all with some kind of centre which survived deaths and departures. I met Norman's successor in American Studies, Kai Erikson (son of Erik Erikson, the author of the psychobiography *The Young Luther*) and went to some seminars in his department, which I have now forgotten. Forgotten, too, until my old letters reminded me, was lunch with Charles Feidelson of the Yale English Department, and with Daniel Aaron, visiting from Harvard. Were there any Yale women? If so, I didn't meet any.

Compared with other university towns, such as Cambridge, England or Cambridge, Massachusetts, New Haven was dull, but there were bright patches. In Yale's astonishing art gallery, on Saturday afternoons after the

Beinecke closed, I discovered many treasures donated by Yale alumni, which showed the New England heritage, its wealth as well as its cultural history. Its collection of early American silver included John Winthrop's chocolate pot and Ezra Stiles' sugar bowl; there was some wonderful colonial furniture and among the European paintings were a Van Gogh and a Cézanne, donated by Henry Luce, and a Manet and a Corot, gifts from John Hay Whitney.

This world of inherited wealth and privilege, expressed in the Yale University Art Gallery, was the one into which Edith Wharton was born in 1862. The daughter of the best dressed woman in New York, she was meagrely educated by governesses. Her father's library was her main resource. Her first attempt at fiction, written when she was eleven, began: '"Oh, how do you do, Mrs Brown?" said Mrs Tompkins. "If only I had known you were going to call I should have tidied up the drawing-room."' Her mother glanced at the first lines and remarked dismissively: 'Drawing-rooms are always tidy'.[2] At twenty-three, Edith married Teddy Wharton, an affable Bostonian with whom she had nothing in common except a love of travel. Slowly and tentatively, knowing nothing of the world of books, she began to publish short stories and novels. At her first meeting with Henry James, she was too shy to speak to the great man, but their friendship became one of the most important in her life and perhaps in his too. Like James she was an expatriate. She divorced Teddy Wharton in 1913 and made her permanent home in France.

Wharton's first big success *The House of Mirth,* published in 1905 when she was forty-three, was a sharp satiric attack on the New York in which she had grown up. *The Age of Innocence* (1920) begins in the 1870s, the time of her childhood. Gentler in tone than *The House of Mirth*, it has been read as wholly nostalgic. When it won the Pulitzer Prize (given for the novel that 'best presents the wholesome atmosphere of American life and the highest standard of American manners and manhood') Wharton was indignant. Irony, she said, must have become as unintelligible as Chinese if her work could be so misread. Yet the impression of that novel as an unambiguous celebration of the hero's self-sacrifice remained. I thought it was more complicated than that, and had put the case in a thesis chapter called 'Prufrock in Brownstone'. My external examiner, Blake Nevius of the University of California at Los Angeles, author of the standard critical work on Wharton, had rather grumpily conceded in his report that I had scored a few points. I would need more than that for a new book; and the manuscripts seemed a good place to start.

Exploring the Wharton papers, I looked first at the author's manuscript revisions: the handwritten corrections and deletions that marked various stages of a novel's growth. Inevitably, because I was immersed in the Lewis biography, I turned to the letters and notebooks, first for more light on the chosen novels, but soon because the author's life interested me more and more, I began to order boxes of correspondence in which Wharton's publishing career could be traced—the progress of 'Lady into Author' as one writer described it.[3] I looked at figures which showed her earnings, and letters in which she dealt, with increasingly confident briskness, with her publishers. The archive was extensive, with more than 50 000 items. It contained letters from expatriate Americans such as Henry James and Bernard Berenson, and from childhood friends who had stayed at home, like Sara Norton, the talented daughter of Harvard's Professor Charles Eliot Norton. Tantalisingly, Wharton's letters to her manipulative journalist lover Morton Fullerton, quoted by Lewis, are not in this collection. Yet the letters in the Beinecke have a satisfying range of variety and tone. Anyone who believed in the public self that Wharton presented would pause at the multiple selves they reveal. Delivered ceremoniously to my desk, in dark blue boxes tied with gold ribbon, the Wharton papers made me understand how scholars could contentedly spend ten years or a working lifetime on a single project.

Although the New York of Edith Wharton's early years had long ago been displaced by the modern city, some evocative fragments remained. The scenes and places I was discovering in Lewis's biography and in the Beinecke boxes soon became visible. During the Thanksgiving holiday in November, and on several other weekends, I went to New York, to stay with my cousin John Gorman who after twenty expatriate years in medical research was a brilliant guide to the city, old and new. His apartment on East 56th Street, with dazzling views of the Manhattan lights, was my first experience of high-rise living. Walking with his young children in Central Park, or gazing at the Fifth Avenue mansions and dilapidated brownstones of the Lower East Side, I began to see Edith Wharton's world. Lewis's biography had drawn the map; and the scenes of *The House of Mirth* and *The Age of Innocence* took on physical reality, as did those of her reticent autobiography, *A Backward Glance*.

The visible remnants of nineteenth-century New York in the modern city were matched in the Beinecke collection of photographs. Edith Wharton, whose first book was *The Decoration of Houses*, was passionately interested in domestic architecture and design. Houses, in her fiction, are powerful expressions of the self, and the houses in which she chose to live, from Lenox, Massachusetts to Paris and Hyères, evoke her personality. I'd been puzzled by Lewis's choice of a jacket photograph of Edith Wharton. Not seated at her ease, but standing, not facing the camera but looking down as she reads a letter, formally dressed with hair piled high, she looks grimly determined, like a nineteenth-century actress doing Lady Macbeth's big scene. The files of photographs showed that Lewis chose as well as anyone could. Shadowed under weighty Edwardian hats, or stiffly posed as author for a publicity shot at her uncluttered desk, Wharton never gave the cameras a chance. Henry James called her 'The Firebird' or 'The Angel of Devastation', images of power which are belied in the photographs. Again and again, an awkward pose, an evasively turned head, suggest the extreme shyness of the reserved, underconfident woman she always claimed to be.

My choice of Edith Wharton as a thesis topic at ANU had been taken without much thought. Henry James, my first preference, was an overworked area; and from James it was an easy progression to the younger writer who was often seen, mistakenly, as his disciple. Reading her papers at Yale, I began to see a personal connection in her way of showing the cobwebs of customs, the virtues and constraints of a small, narrow society. Wharton's characters have a complex fate. Wanting liberty and independence, they feel the seductive charm of an ordered world. In her own lifetime, Wharton said, 'what had seemed unalterable rules of conduct became of a sudden observances as quaintly arbitrary as the domestic rites of the Pharoahs'.[4] As the chronicler of these observances, she found them endearing as well as absurd, and she valued the probity of the life they represented. Her trapped characters are not always sure that they want to escape.

There was a good deal in my ordered childhood world that was arbitrarily constraining—most obviously the pious practices and prohibitions of a convent education that hadn't changed since my grandmother's time. Catholic Kew of my childhood had arbitrary rules as well as moral certainties, and these were often confused. Wharton's late development as a writer had obvious meaning for me. I wouldn't claim her as a role model—the discrepancies in time and place, talent and achievement were immeasurable—but as I read her own account of her life as a young woman in a highly structured society, I felt some degree of connection. Unexpectedly, with the imperious Edith, I found something of the empathy a biographer needs to feel with her subject.

As the autumn turned to winter in New Haven I knew that I was spending too much time on biographical material. I had never thought of writing a life. As a student at Melbourne University in the early 1950s, I was not interested in biography. No one was. We were all New Critics in the making; and the close reading of the text was what it was all about. The space for biography in English Department lectures was minimal. In the first three minutes, while students were settling down, rummaging for pens and notebooks, the lecturer would give a brief outline: just enough to make sure we knew that Jane Austen was not a Victorian novelist, and not to mix her up with Jane Eyre. No one took much notice of this information; and although a lecturer would mention the title of the standard life of the author, it would be a rare student who thought to take it off the shelf. Biography, it was understood, was the sort of thing best left to the History Department. It was factual, not imaginative. It might lead to the dangerous waters of the intentional fallacy, and besides, we didn't need it.

In this context, even in the mid-1970s, it would have been adventurous to drop my critical study of Edith Wharton and embark on a biography to challenge that of R.W.B. Lewis. And yet, as I untied the golden ribbons on box after box of the Beinecke manuscript collection, that is what I would have liked to do. Losing interest in the ideas of my thesis, losing confidence in its having much to say, I wavered. Critical study or biography? Home to Australia, with its close personal connections, and to Monash, which offered far more satisfaction and enjoyment than Yale? Or a planned return to Yale, with a distant prospect of completing a scholarly work for an international readership. Small world, big world. What did I really want?

If Norman Holmes Pearson had lived, it might have been different. He had thought it a good moment for a critical study, and had offered to talk to a commissioning editor at Yale University Press. With his close knowledge of R.W.B. Lewis's work on Wharton, Norman was well placed to judge my chances. Not that he had actually read my thesis. He took it on trust from Grahame Johnston, its first examiner at ANU, whom he had met in Canberra before visiting Monash. The invitation to Yale was as much Grahame's idea as Norman's. For years he had been urging me to be more adventurous, and above all to start publishing. Why was there such a gap, he asked, between the assurance of my writing, and my 'demure and diffident' manner with senior academics—even those whose work he knew I didn't in the least admire. 'Don't be intimidated by those chaps', he would say, briskly dismissing a world of eminent scholars. 'Most of them can't write nearly as well as you do.' When Grahame commissioned my first book, *Martin Boyd*, for the Oxford

University Press series *Australian Writers and their Work*, he thought of this brief study of an expatriate Australian writer as the forerunner of a more ambitious work on the expatriate American Edith Wharton. Against his expectations and my own, it would lead eventually to a Boyd biography and a move from American to Australian literature. Published in 1974, the year before I went to Yale, it clinched my promotion to a senior lectureship.

In the long evenings at New Haven I thought about the surprising ways in which my career had seemed to shape itself without much planning on my part. At a time when women seldom reached the higher levels, I had done well, especially for a latecomer. The Monash English Department had a better representation of women than its counterparts elsewhere in Australia. Few in number (four out of twenty tenured staff in the late 1960s) they were individually influential. Jenny Strauss was an eloquent policy-maker whose views in staff meetings and on university committees carried more weight than those of most of the men. Margery Morgan, an outstanding Shaw scholar from Britain, was promoted from a senior lectureship to Reader in the mid-1960s. Elaine Barry's intellectually demanding and imaginative American Literature courses won her an Associate Professorship in 1975. Such successes were rare at the time. Leonie Kramer, Professor of Australian Literature at the University of Sydney, was the exception in reaching the top level. Most women, at least until the 1980s, clustered at the lower levels, as tutors and lecturers. A senior lectureship in 1975 was a good outcome for me; and for many years I was happy to leave it at that. Promotion to Reader wasn't so easy to get, and came later, when I had a record of publications.

In the long evenings at New Haven, contrasting sociable Monash with unreachable Yale, I wasn't sure how much I really wanted the Wharton project, if it meant long stretches of time away from home. The Yale collection was the most important of the Wharton papers, but there were papers in Indiana, at Harvard and elsewhere which I would have needed for any serious biographical approach. Permissions from the literary executors of the Wharton estate would be essential: how would an unknown Australian negotiate them? I thought of Herman Melville's prayer, when he was writing *Moby Dick*, for Time, Strength, Cash and Patience. It was hard to see when I could get back to the United States. I couldn't move to and fro between teaching terms as British scholars did.

On the morning of 12 November 1975, I overheard part of a conversation from the next table in the hotel dining room. 'I see the Australians fired their President', one said, folding his *New York Times*. 'A pity it wasn't as easy for us.' I understood the reference to the slow process of removing Richard Nixon from the White House a year earlier, but it was the first I'd heard of the removal of the Whitlam government in Canberra; and it came as a reminder of the gap in time and space. Two weeks later, a solitary dinner in the hotel dining room on my forty-fifth birthday was a reminder of what an itinerant academic's future might be. I'd been away almost the whole year, with nine months in Cambridge, England, before moving on to Yale. It was time to go home and as the New England winter closed in I booked a mid-December flight to Melbourne, with some regrets for the biographical impulse I was leaving behind.

That impulse flickered a little in the following year. In August 1976, during a conference of the Australian and New Zealand American Studies Association, held at Monash, I met Leon Edel, author of the celebrated five-volume biography of Henry James, who was our most distinguished visitor. I won Edel's friendship by rescuing him from a noisy motel in Carlton and resettling him in the sedate luxury of the Windsor Hotel, where James himself would have been at home. Awestruck at first—driving Henry James would have felt much the same—I drove Edel to and from the conference every day, heard about his work in progress on the Bloomsbury Group, and told him about my New Haven disappointment. Edel, a trim, courtly seventy-year-old, recalled his youth in 1930s Paris, when he had met the famous and formidable Edith Wharton, not long before her death. He thought I should persevere with a book about her, and pointed out that Lewis's biography made it easier because all the basic work was done. I would be free to choose my own line. Her ghost stories, he suggested, might be a promising way into psychobiography. Our talks during the conference week revived the possibilities of publication, with Leon Edel the guide to the American scene, as Norman Holmes Pearson would have been.

After returning to the University of Hawaii, Edel sent me a copy of his *Literary Biography* with a friendly letter repeating his offer of help and his department's hospitality during whatever Wharton travels I might undertake. In stately Jamesian prose he sent his thanks and appreciation of the 'mutuality and fine scholarly reciprocities' of his Monash visit. I still have the book, with the letter folded inside it, but I didn't visit Edel at the Institute of Biographical Studies at Hawaii, or in London, where he was finishing his Bloomsbury group biography, *A House of Lions.* His letter coincided with the death of Grahame Johnston in Canberra. This was as sudden as Norman's death, and sadder. Aged only forty-seven, Grahame had just published a major work and taken up a new appointment as deputy director of the Humanities Research Centre. He and Norman Holmes Pearson had been the architects of the Wharton enterprise. The two deaths, scarcely more than a year apart, seemed finally to close that door, and for all Leon Edel's warmth and his immense international prestige, I didn't want to reopen it. Much later, Edel's ideas about biography came to mind, when I was ready for them.

II

Border Crossings

5

Matching the Matriarchs: Ethel Turner and Mary Grant Bruce

In an academic's life, research and teaching should go hand in hand. That's the conventional wisdom, but as I re-read my diary for 1978 I can see myself leading a double life. Here I am, measuring my weeks with *The Scarlet Letter* and *Moby Dick*; struggling with *Leaves of Grass*, rejoicing when we reach the 1880s and it's time for *Huckleberry Finn* and *Portrait of a Lady*. Bored with Hemingway, enthralled with Fitzgerald—so the year passes with the great works of American literature presumably my main occupation. But every Wednesday and nearly every Sunday, there's a change of focus. Nothing canonical here: I am reading *Mates at Billabong*, *Little*

Mother Meg, *Captain Jim* and *Captain Cub*, and other works by Ethel Turner and Mary Grant Bruce, at the rate of three or four a day on Wednesdays, and spending Sunday mornings in the State Library of Victoria searching the Children's Page of the *Leader* weekly magazine from 1900 to 1910. I am looking for anything signed 'Cinderella', or 'MGB', which will be the work of a young journalist, Minnie Bruce, later known as Mary Grant Bruce, the author of the Billabong books. As 'Cinderella', Bruce ran competitions for the best letter from the under-tens, gave instructions ('For Busy Hands') on tying useful knots or making book-stands, divulged 'Queer Things about Ants', recalled 'How I kept Poultry'. Her 1901 column marking the death of Queen Victoria unconvincingly evoked the young Victoria as 'a loving, merry-hearted mother, romping with her little ones'. As an alternative to *Moby Dick* (even the whaling chapters) my new direction seems a bit extreme.

That new direction led to my first full-length book based on Australian texts and archival sources. The La Trobe Library's manuscript collection at the State Library of Victoria was my first Australian archive. My project, which first appeared as an entertainment, was a backward journey to the books of my childhood, the novels of Ethel Turner and Mary Grant Bruce. Not just my childhood, or that of my sisters: these were the books my mother and my aunt read before the First World War. In the 1970s my nieces seemed almost equally absorbed in a world long gone by. What could this new generation find in *Seven Little Australians* and the Billabong books? My brother Hugh had been reading Richard Usborne's *Clubland Heroes*, a wry, satiric study of the very English adventures created by John Buchan, 'Sapper' of the *Bulldog Drummond* books, and the zany Dornford Yates. He thought I could do something equally amusing and revealing with Australian girls' books of the same period. With no scholarly project in mind, and at a loss, after my Yale disappointment, to see a new direction, I was tempted by the idea of writing for a general readership. It was obvious to both of us that Turner and Bruce were the only possibilities. Hugh supplied an irreverent title, *Seven Little Billabongs*; and within a few days of our conversation I was engrossed in this unlikely literary project. Instead of grappling with Lacan and Derrida, as my colleagues were doing in this decade of literary theory, in which deconstruction was displacing close reading, I became eccentrically engaged in re-reading the complete novels of Turner and Bruce, all seventy-eight of them. I had left this world behind when I was no more than twelve but my recall was almost perfect.

Retrieving the books was the first step. My nieces gave back the battered copies which had survived the generations, and bookshops had a few reprints. Discovering that municipal libraries had discarded most of them as old-fashioned, sexist, imperialist, racist—as no doubt they would prove to be—I began to think about the Australia in which these books were written, and about the extraordinary continuity of values which kept the works of Turner and Bruce in print from 1894, when *Seven Little Australians* was published, to 1942 when the last of the Billabong books appeared.

Soon I had a complete set of the books. Convents were great conservers of the past; and I raided the FCJ Vaucluse Convent in Richmond (sister school of Genazzano) for about forty books which had been removed from the library shelves but not yet disposed of. Family and friends supplied the rest. Many were in the editions I remembered. *Seven Little Australians* had somehow survived in its late Victorian binding, in dark red covers with gilt lettering and a title-page vignette of the death of Judy Woolcot carefully glued back into place. Other early Turner novels had been rebound in dismal bottle-green oilcloth with titles printed in white ink, but their line drawings of little girls in pinafores and boys in sailor suits held their period charm. The first Billabong books were visually pleasing too. The 1911 frontispiece of *Mates at Billabong* shows Norah Linton gazing devotedly at her pony. She wears the divided skirt that was then comparatively modern, even daring (many women still rode side-saddle) but her long well-brushed curls are as reassuringly feminine as the love of music on which her author insists.

Between *Seven Little Australians* in 1894 and *Billabong Riders* in 1942, every year brought a new novel by Turner or Bruce, or one from each, as a Christmas present or a prize day award for Australian children. The two became rivals during the First World War period with parallel stories of heroes in khaki: *Captain Cub* (1917) and *Captain Jim* (1919). Ethel Turner retired in 1928 but Bruce continued to produce at least one book a year for another fourteen years. By 1942 the complete works of these two writers were available to give Australian children images of themselves, their society, their immediate and their more distant past. Turner's early fiction mirrored the depression of the 1890s and the departure of the Bush Contingent to fight in the Boer War in 1900. Bruce, who had written about the first telephones and motor cars in Victoria, took her readers through the depression of the 1930s to Pearl Harbor and the war against Japan. Between them they dominated the juvenile market in Australia for more than fifty years. Turner's *Seven Little Australians* was the most spectacular single success. Staged, filmed, televised and translated, and reprinted at least forty-five times, it would be hard to think of any Australian novel which is so widely known. Bruce's success was cumulative. The fifteen Billabong books collectively were a publishing phenomenon to equal Turner's record.

As I began to re-read the novels and to explore the author's lives, I could see patterns of sameness and contrast. Both women were born in the 1870s; both died in 1958. The same publisher, Ward, Lock of London, brought out their novels in a uniform edition which, as Ethel Turner complained, made them look as alike as 'tins of jam'. Their material was family life in Australia, seen by Turner from the perspective of suburban Sydney and by Bruce from that of the Victorian outback.

In strengths and weaknesses they complemented one another. Turner's skill in characterisation was balanced by Bruce's neatly constructed plots. For adventure with a guaranteed happy ending, Bruce was always reliable, while Turner's domestic comedy and melodrama sometimes ended in tears.

Turner's readership was mainly female. The *Bulletin* recommended her work to 'girls … fluttering a brief and tremulous gown at the meeting of the calf and ankle'. The Billabong books were read by boys as well as girls. In Bruce's patriarchal world there was no place for romantic flutterings. Although her heroine Norah Linton, first encountered as a ten-year-old in *A Little Bush Maid* (1910) was eventually brought to marriage and motherhood, sex had nothing to do with it. 'I'm marrying my mate', Norah said, in the ninth Billabong book, before departing on a honeymoon camping excursion with Wally Meadows, her brother's best friend. Their one child, Davie, was born between volumes.

The Turner and Bruce novels had a special importance for Australian children. Before the 1950s, as Ivan Southall remarked, there was almost no juvenile fiction set in Australia. 'Good things, that parents would buy for you, came from England … Australia never earned a mention except as the wilderness to which profligate cousins were sent and out of which lost uncles came.'[1] Herbert Evatt, future leader of the Australian Labor Party, remembering his early reading, before the First World War, described *Seven Little Australians* as a revelation: 'the real miracle to myself was that it could be exciting and real *and* Australian ... here was the Sydney and the country I knew ...'[2] When I read them in the 1930s, they were the only Australian books for children that had any importance for me. Our farm holidays at Tallarook and my passion for riding were in the spirit of the Billabong books. Among the Turner novels, I remember returning to a little-known title, *In the Mist of the Mountains,* to re-read a beguiling chapter in which four children write stories which they show to their neighbour, a famous author. He sends the stories to a printer, who transforms them into four 'real books', printed and bound, with the children's names as authors in gilt lettering. As a ten-year-old, I couldn't have said whether Norah Linton's new pony or the Lomax children's precocious publications were more enticing, but I'm sure that the Australian settings made them real, as English books were not.

As I worked my way through box after box of Turner and Bruce novels, I could see any number of questions to ask. Whatever their literary merits, these books had given acceptable versions of self to three generations of Australian children. Images of city and country, nationalism, war and imperial loyalties, ideas about race and class, were all explored with utter certainty. These authors knew their public—and so did the London publishers for whom Turner and Bruce were valuable literary properties. I began to think about the context in which they wrote, about their publishing history, their sales and marketing, their sense of audience—all these inseparable from questions about the authors themselves. Who were they, and how had they shaped their remarkable careers? I went in search of Ethel Turner and Mary Grant Bruce.

Having learned some lessons from my Archbishop Mannix interviews, I looked first at manuscript sources. Turner and Bruce, symmetrical in life as in work, each had two children, and each was survived by one son, who held the copyright in the literary estates. I would need the approval of Jonathan Bruce in Melbourne and Sir Adrian Curlewis in Sydney, but those approaches could wait. My first experience of working with manuscripts in an Australian library didn't match Yale's Beinecke Library in luxurious surroundings, nor were the papers so exquisitely catalogued, so reverentially presented, as the Wharton papers had been. Yet from the first day there were exhilarating moments of discovery. The Bruce Papers in the La Trobe Library, State Library of Victoria, were thin, with only just enough personal material to make a biographical chapter on the reticent author of the Billabong books. By contrast, the Turner Papers in the Mitchell Library, State Library of New South Wales, overflowed with diaries, letters, manuscripts and photographs of the ebullient Ethel: more than enough for a full-scale biography if I had wanted to write it. But the idea of a double portrait was working so well, from my readings of the published texts and the primary sources, that I never seriously thought of changing direction.

I had to work harder on Bruce, coaxing her to emerge from the few private letters, making sure that she was not extinguished by her livelier, more gifted but less reliable rival. The two careers would be the main focus.

Ethel and Minnie—I soon began to call them by their familiar names—could have been made for one another: they fitted together as neatly as two halves of a jigsaw puzzle. The English-born Turner claimed suburban Sydney as the background for her stories of creative, naughty children. When Judy Woolcot, the rebellious heroine of *Seven Little Australians,* is killed by a falling tree during an outback holiday, the tragedy suggests Turner's nervous dread of the untamed Australia she never visited. Bruce, a country-town girl born in Sale, Victoria, placed paradise in the cattle station named Billabong, and hell in the city of boarding schools and cigarette-smoking moral weaklings. Turner's little larrikins and moody anti-heroes find trouble within the self. Bruce's laconic bush children, challenged by the natural world, win through because of their unreflecting courage.

Both women were ambitious professional writers whose career aims were deflected by unexpected early success in a story for children. Turner thought of *Seven Little Australians* as a trifling piece of work, not to be compared with some 'great work' of adult fiction in which she hoped to make her name. 'Killed Judy to slow music', she wrote irreverently after finishing the scene for which she won enduring fame. Tears flowed for Judy Woolcot, generation after generation, as they had flowed for Dickens' Little Nell. Astute enough to refuse her publisher's offer to buy the rights of her novel, Turner was nevertheless astonished at the golden shower of royalties that followed. When she was asked for a sequel, Turner unwillingly produced *The Family at Misrule* (1896), a second novel about the Woolcot family of *Seven Little Australians. Little Mother Meg* appeared in 1902, and as late as 1928, *Judy and Punch* filled in a missing year in the life of Judy Woolcot. For the rest of her long writing life, Turner struggled and compromised, unwilling to lose her popularity or her income, but impatient with the need to keep in mind the sensibilities of the young person. Her 'great work' was never written.

I had become interested in publishing history at Yale, while reading Edith Wharton's letters to her publishers. There were similar treasures in the Turner archive, which holds correspondence between the young author and William Steele, Ward, Lock's Australian representative, who liked to be called the 'godfather of Seven Little Australians'. Proud of his discovery, perhaps a little in love with the pretty, vivacious young author, and increasingly possessive of her talent, Steele kept a sharp eye on her for the occasional waywardness of her characters, their breaches of decorum, and the Australian slang for which he blamed her association with the Sydney *Bulletin*. Steele reminded Turner of the importance of the English market. 'Rowdiness' might be tolerated in Sydney but it would not do in London. She was rebuked by the *Sydney Morning Herald*'s reviewer for Pip Woolcot's exclamation: 'My oath!' This was replaced in the second and subsequent editions by 'My word!' Editorial decisions made by Ward, Lock in London often infuriated Turner, but distance was against her. By the time her protests reached the editorial desk it was too late. She was 'wildly angry' at having the 'namby-pamby title' of *Mother's Little Girl* imposed on one of her novels. A reference to divorce in *The Little Larrikin* prompted some editorial pruning in which the offending character vanished, without reference to the author.

The Turner archive was a wonderful source of insight into the author's personality and ambitions. It also opened up more general questions about the Anglo-Australian publishing relationship and the changing notions of what was permissible for a juvenile readership. There was nothing comparable in the Bruce Papers. Turner, who spent her entire writing life in Sydney, kept copies of her own letters and the replies. Bruce, an expatriate for many years, had no settled home and died in England, leaving few papers of any kind. Her relationship with her publishers seems likely to have been more serene than Turner's, but there was no way of being certain. When I wrote to Ward, Lock, in the hope of retrieving the Bruce correspondence, I was disappointed to find that all their records had been destroyed in the bombing of London during the Second World War.

The sources were similarly uneven for the private lives. Turner's diary overflowed with emotion. Charles Cope, her mother's third husband, who seems to have been in love with his stepdaughter, made tremendous scenes. 'He says he would far rather bury me than give me to any man ... after Mother he loved me better than anyone on earth ... he should have the same abhorrence to any man', Turner wrote. Her refusal to return a kiss from Mr Cope provoked fury: 'He declares he won't speak to me again this side of the grave'.[3] Tears flowed, voices were raised, doors slammed. Turner's happy marriage with barrister Herbert Curlewis followed indecision, the huffy return of love letters, rapturous reconciliations. Moving from this highly theatrical household to that of Mary Grant Bruce brought a sharp drop in emotional temperature.

At thirty-four, after years of independence as a professional journalist, Bruce married her second cousin, George Bruce, a British Army officer who wrote adventure stories. One or two affectionate and thoughtful letters survive to show that he fostered her career. Mary Grant Bruce doesn't seem to have fretted at the limits of the juvenile market. She said that she was more or less forced by fan letters and her publisher's pressure to marry off Norah to Wally, but 'beyond that I drew the line'. There is nothing in her fiction to match Turner's urge to show the realities of love, marriage and motherhood, and the countervailing demands of a career. Turner wrote in the Victorian domestic tradition. Her main literary debts are to England's Charlotte Yonge of *The Daisy Chain* and the American Louisa Alcott for *Little Women*. Bruce's early reading favoured boys' adventure stories, and her emotional range doesn't go beyond asexual ('boyish') heroines like those of John Buchan.

I would have liked to know whether it was Bruce's own widening sympathies or pressure from publishers and readers that modified the racism of the early Billabong books, but there was no evidence either way. She had begun to write at a time when Australians unselfconsciously used 'white man' as a term of praise, as in 'Thanks, Boss, you're a real white man'. Poets like Lawson and Paterson associated the Chinese with dirt and disease. The *Bulletin* summed up: 'We know the Chinese better than most. He produces two things, vice and vegetables.' The image of the Aborigine in popular fiction was either that of a savage, or a domestic pet like Billabong's Black Billy. Bruce's racist stereotypes in her early novels were patronising but benign. Unlike such writers of adventure stories as her English contemporaries 'Sapper' or John Buchan, she has no slimy Portuguese villains nor evil Chinese. When crime touches Billabong, the invader is invariably white, and usually lower class. From the early 1920s the Lintons' rouseabout Black Billy and their Chinese gardener Lee Wing become more than caricatures. Still worshipfully keeping their places in the Billabong hierarchy, they play heroic roles. The last novel in the series, *Billabong Riders* includes a tribute to Lee Wing for his 'humour and shrewdness' and 'quiet, gentle manner'. Jim Linton, formerly convinced that the Aborigines are 'the lowest form of civilisation', rebukes a drover for speaking of 'dirty miserable brutes'. 'We took their country', Jim says. 'I reckon we owe them something.' Aboriginal culture, he now believes, is 'a deeper thing than we can understand'.

I missed my chance to ask questions about these changes when I visited Bruce's surviving son. Jonathan Bruce, a very intelligent man with a keen sense of irony, might have spoken frankly about his mother's views if I had asked the right questions. Not 'when did your mother stop being a racist?', but something less confronting, might have opened up the topic. Jonathan Bruce spoke with humour and detachment about the Billabong books, which he saw as money-spinners, well written and neatly plotted, but with no literary pretensions. He was amused to be asked if his own childhood matched that of his mother's novels. Absolutely not. For one thing, much of it had been spent in Ireland, where his father's regiment was stationed, in 1920s Melbourne, where his mother resumed her work as a journalist, and at Bexhill-on-Sea, in England. Mary Grant Bruce did not share the Lintons' passion for outback Australia. Although she had learned a good deal about cattle station life from holidays at her uncle's property, she was always an outsider there. A clever country-town girl who won the Shakespeare Society prize three times, she was eager to move to Melbourne and later to London. Readers of the Billabong books are constantly reminded of the close relationship between physical and moral wellbeing, but Billabong's creator, a chain smoker, broke a basic rule. Good humour and good cooking are likewise part of the Billabong style. The Lintons' cook, Brownie, presides over a sociable place, which offers a round-the-clock supply of pikelets, hot scones and cups of tea as well as the huge, delicious meals sent to the Lintons' dining table. For Mary Grant Bruce and her family, it was nothing like that. According to Jonathan Bruce, his mother was a hopelessly incompetent cook, who chose to live for some years in a series of boarding houses. She belonged to Melbourne's Lyceum Club for professional women and was perfectly at home in the city. If Norah Linton was her alternative childhood self, that self was soon outgrown.

At the time of my visit to him in 1978 Jonathan Bruce was well aware that his mother's books were under attack. Teachers and librarians were horrified at the racial attitudes of the early novels, and all of them were being removed from the shelves of school and municipal libraries. The novels were also in trouble for their class assumptions and their unquestioning loyalty to monarchy and Empire. This form of censorship is understandable. Juvenile fiction has always been monitored according to the current ideas of what is good for children, but it is possible that the campaign to take Billabong off the map did not do justice to a child's capacity to discern false or outdated values in a book set in the past. The trouble with censorship of this kind is that it removes evidence that should be confronted, and placed in historical context. The huge popularity of the Billabong books during the first half of the twentieth century was an important measure of national feeling. Bruce's reputation sank while the works of her like-minded contemporaries, Henry Lawson, Banjo Paterson and Miles Franklin, were almost immune from criticism. My chapters on the Billabong books were ironic rather than indignant. This got me into trouble from both sides. Some readers sensed betrayal of their childhood idols. I had letters complaining about my 'sarcastic' tone. Others thought me irresponsible in failing to urge the censors on. Jonathan Bruce wrote to thank me for the 'gentle treatment of my most uncomplicated mother'. And he loved the flippant, portmanteau title *Seven Little Billabongs*.

Still keeping to their places in the Australian topography, the Bruces lived in Mount Eliza, not far from Melbourne, while Ethel Turner's son Sir Adrian Curlewis, a retired judge, had a harbour view at Mosman. Charmed and excited by the Turner Papers in the Mitchell Library, I very nearly said yes when Sir Adrian asked if I would be interested in writing his mother's biography. I wasn't sure whether this offer would depend on my dropping the double Turner–Bruce portrait, and I didn't ask. I could see that he was not pleased by my linking the two women in a way which made them seem equal in talents and importance. He was right to rate his mother's work above the Billabong books, at least in literary terms, but I sensed a reverence in the Mosman air that might mean trouble. Not that there was anything in his mother's life to evade or gloss over. Turner's lively intelligence, her humour and generosity, and the ups and downs of her remarkable career, would have made her an excellent biographical subject—much better than Bruce whose personal reserve matched her scanty archive. Turner was far more venturesome. Although her novels seldom stray from the domestic scene, they show the turmoil of family life. Their sentimentality co-exists with a shrewd sense of the contradictions of personality. Bruce's Lintons, forever perfect, never changing, need an adventure to set them moving. Turner's ambitious young women have ideas about themselves and the world. Feminist and socialist ideas are explored, and although the resolution confirms the traditional values of home, motherhood and suburban middle-class life, the aspiring heroine is taken seriously.

Sir Adrian's question—which was not quite an invitation—made me think once more about writing a biography. In the Australian context Turner was important. Her papers opened up interesting questions about the publishing scene at the turn of the century and the Anglo-Australian relationship. They documented the tensions which most Australian writers felt, at a time when a London publisher was the measure of success, as well as a source of control which was often irksome. Henry Lawson told Miles Franklin in 1902 that if she were to change from Blackwoods (who published *My Brilliant Career*) to Angus and Robertson of Sydney, 'it would be a big come-down from a leading British publisher to an Australian one—no matter how big the latter'.[4]

In 1897 Turner's close friend, Louise Mack, sent *Teens, A Story of Australian Schoolgirls* to Angus and Robertson, and later regretted it. She would probably have done better to have joined Turner and Bruce on the Ward, Lock list. Presumably because of Turner's triumph, Angus and Robertson presented *Teens* in a format identical with that of *Seven Little Australians*: a handsome three-and-sixpence-worth in red cloth and gilt. Its sales were disappointing; and although Mack carried out Turner's ambition of moving to London, she never had the big success both young women had dreamed of in their time together at Sydney Girls' High School. By staying at home, reluctantly accepting the limits of the juvenile market, Turner had the best of the Australian market as well as good English sales and many translations in Europe.

I left Mosman quite sure that Ethel Turner's son was a keeper of the flame with whom any biographer would have to walk warily. Sir Adrian was interested in my suggestion that the diaries should be edited for publication; and this was soon in the hands of his daughter Philippa Poole. After *Seven Little Billabongs* appeared, I had a testy letter from Mrs Poole, to say how much she and her father disliked the title, which they thought trivialised Turner's work. They were displeased, too, at the degree to which I had drawn on the diaries. I replied in equally frosty tones. I didn't then have much sympathy with their response. Ethel Turner, who often turned an ironist's gaze on her own work, would surely have been amused. 'I do want Fame—plenty of it', she said, and she paid the price in countless saccharine interviews. Wasn't a little irony overdue? Later, when I gave more thought to the problems faced by family members in trying to interpret the presumed wishes of the dead, I felt some regrets. Not for the title, which caught the critics' attention and was just right for the mood of the book, but for my own failure to consider the Curlewis point of view. They were right to see Turner's literary intelligence as superior to that of Mary Grant Bruce. And although my chapters showed the difference in quality between the two authors, the title did suggest the 'tins of jam' likeness that Turner had found so annoying.

The Curlewis rebuke confirmed my doubts about a Turner biography. The divided readership was one problem. When the Turner novels first appeared, they had a wide appeal, to children, young girls, even adults. In the 1980s the potential readers of *Seven Little Australians* would have been under ten. There were no flappers to read Turner's 'flapperature' as the *Bulletin* described it. Who then would read a serious life of Turner or Bruce? Alison Alexander's *Billabong's Author* (1979) and Sandy Yarwood's *From a Chair in the Sun: a Life of Ethel Turner* (1994) were solidly researched but burdened by the domestic trivia which only a devoted fan would enjoy. And the fan club had long since grown up, grown old, died. Women of my generation liked *Seven Little Billabongs* because it combined a nostalgia trip with the rediscovery (amused, but sometimes appalled) of their younger selves. Judging from their responses, these readers were more interested in musing about their own youthful identification with Norah Linton than in getting to know her creator. *Seven Little Billabongs*, with its brief biographical chapters and its affectionately ironic tone, seemed to work. I followed it in 1984 with *Australia Through the Looking Glass: Children's Fiction 1830–1980* for which I did the research in collaboration with my historian sister Frances O'Neill. As Australian social history and publishing history, this was fun to write, and it did something to fill a very large gap.

The growing academic interest in Australian literature in the 1970s and 1980s was not matched by attention to children's books. This was demonstrated in 1987, when I had an urgent, apologetic phone call from University of Queensland academic Laurie Hergenhan, general editor of the *New Penguin History of Australian Literature*, asking me to write something on Australian children's literature for this important project, timed for the bicentennial year. Thirty-three essays had been commissioned, and most were already completed. As I wrote my essay at high speed to meet the deadline, I was reminded of the precarious status of 'kiddylit', as it was patronisingly known among academics. The new literary history claimed to be inclusive. It denounced the 'canon formation' of the 1960s. It commissioned essays on melodrama and romance, on humour, war literature, utopian fiction. But until bibliographer John Arnold went to work on the final section, 'Sources for the Study of Australian Literature' and was reminded of *Seven Little Billabongs,* no one on the editorial committee noticed the gap. No Turner or Bruce, no *Magic Pudding* (except briefly, under Humour), no Banksia Men or Ginger Meggs. In a chapter on publishing, nothing about the 1950s renaissance in Australian children's fiction under Frank Eyre of Oxford University Press. No one had noticed Ivan Southall's international triumph with the Carnegie Medal in 1971, or Patricia Wrightson's Hans Christian Andersen Medals. Cramming them all into my twelve pages, I concluded that in the garden of Australian literature, children's books were confined to a very small sandpit.

Pluralist as always, the Monash English department was never patronising about 'Ethel and Minnie'. I still have the little Swedish glass penguin given to me by the head of department David Bradley at an impromptu departmental party when Penguin Books, having bought the paperback rights from Melbourne University Press, published a reprint in 1980. Reviews on first publication in 1979 were good. They ranged from scholarly journals to the *Australian Women's Weekly* which recommended *Seven Little Billabongs* as 'one to put under your Christmas tree'.

Seven Little Billabongs was equally lucky in its publisher. Before I had written the first chapter I had a letter from Peter Ryan, Director of Melbourne University Press, asking for the pleasure of reading an outline of my work-in-progress. He had heard about it, as I later discovered, from two of my Melbourne University friends, George Russell, head of the English Department, and historian Paul Bourke, both of whom were on MUP's board of directors. A contract soon followed; and I then began my close, happy association with MUP and its senior in-house editor, Wendy Sutherland, who thereafter edited all my books. Like Jonathan Bruce, Peter Ryan was amused by the title: 'catchy without being cute', he said. The book caught media attention; and I astonished myself, not only by giving a live-to-air interview on Elizabeth Bond's ABC radio program, but even enjoying this first experience. The lifelong fear of public speaking, which had made me doubt if I could ever lecture, very nearly vanished in the exhilaration of public success with this first book.

Although it began as a diversion, *Seven Little Billabongs* was much more than that. The Turner Papers at the Mitchell Library proved that the pleasures of primary sources were not confined to Yale and other great collections in British and American libraries. One reviewer described *Seven Little Billabongs* as 'scholarly but fun to read'. I saw no contradiction. Unlikely as it now seems, it was *Seven Little Billabongs* that gave me a sense of myself as a writer and the confidence to move outside the academic world to find a general readership. I had always written easily, enjoying the making of a nice phrase, even in my exam papers as a student. Letters home during my travels were a creative outlet for describing people and places, but they were impermanent, forgotten as soon as they were posted. With my first full-length book I discovered the pleasures of shaping ideas, making connections, seeing how each part related to the whole. As each paragraph dropped into place, as each chapter signalled its proper ending, I had an exultant sense of recognition. I was discovering a voice. Ironic comedy was the tone for *Seven Little Billabongs*. Later books would demand other voices and a wider emotional range.

6

Walking upon Ashes: In the Footsteps of Martin Boyd

Biography is not a safe option for a cautious writer. It has its risks and adventures. Samuel Johnson's wonderful metaphor, 'walking upon ashes', suggests the uneasy, shifting ground every biographer treads on when walking into someone else's life. Contemplating the risks of coming close to his own time, Johnson wrote:

> The necessity of complying with times and sparing persons is the great impediment of biography. History may be formed from permanent monuments and records; but lives can only be written from personal knowledge, which is growing every day less and in a short time is lost for ever. What is known can seldom

> be immediately told, and when it might be told it is no longer known. The delicate features of the mind, the nice discrimination of character, and the minute particularities of conduct are soon obliterated; and it is surely better that caprice, obstinacy, frolick and folly, however they might delight in the description, should be silently forgotten, than that, by wanton merriment and unseasonable detection, a pang should be given to a widow, a daughter, a brother or a friend. As the process of these narratives [*The Lives of the Poets*] is now bringing me among my contemporaries, I begin to feel myself *walking upon ashes under which the fire is not extinguished* and coming to the time of which it will be proper to say *nothing that is false rather than all that is true.*[1]

Anyone writing modern biography will share Johnson's sense of unease, though not all will be so sensitive as he was to the feelings of surviving family and friends. But whether the questions of what can be said appear to the biographer as moral scruples or fear of legal constraints, they are always present. And I think the sense we must all share with Johnson—that there are living fires beneath the ashes—is part of the biographical adventure.

Where is the interest if the feeling of a life has gone? We are all eager to feel close to the living fires—although in varying degrees anxious about stepping on hot coals—and if the heat is sometimes alarming, it is also a source of whatever energy the biography may have. There are always choices to be made; and the biographer's decisions about what can be said will be to some extent determined by temperament and the time of writing. What is unsayable in one period of time may become a matter of course within a space as short as a decade or two, according to the ways in which society judges human behaviour.

Call it unseasonable detection, as Johnson does, or romantic quest: every biographer is tempted. We share the dream of discovering evidence that will suddenly and dramatically illuminate the life of the subject: the bundle of letters written in fading ink on yellowing paper, perhaps, the trunk in the attic, the private diary no one knew to have existed. The big dramatic moment in A.S. Byatt's novel *Possession* is the breaking open of a grave, in which the written record of a poet's secret love affair has been hidden. *Possession*, like Henry James' *The Aspern Papers*, raises the moral questions about the rights of the subject—the rights of the dead in these instances. But biography also trespasses on the rights of the living.

It was not until the early 1980s that the chance of writing a full-scale Australian biography first presented itself to me—a life of Martin Boyd, the novelist member of the Boyd family of artists on whose fiction I had already written a short introductory study in the Oxford series *Australian Writers and their Work*. After Boyd's death in Rome in June 1972, a trunkful of his papers and diaries was sent back to Melbourne to his literary executor, his sculptor nephew Guy Boyd. Guy was not sure what to do with Uncle Martin's diaries. He knew that many personal papers had been destroyed, but did the survival of the diaries mean that they were to be spared, or was it his duty to make a bonfire of them? He and his wife Phyllis dutifully set to work, reading diary entries aloud to one another, every evening for a month or so, so as to make sure there was nothing scandalous in them. Their reaction was boredom rather than shock—there was so much trivia about having a haircut, catching a bus on a wet day, losing a bank statement—that sort of thing predominated. There was no reason to destroy these innocuous volumes, nor did they have much literary interest. Having put the diaries aside for some years, Guy Boyd eventually decided that they could go to the National Library, but on restricted access, just in case he'd missed anything.

Before the diaries went to the Library, Guy Boyd allowed me to read them. Because the private self of Martin Boyd was such a surprise, I began to think about a biography. I wasn't immediately drawn to the record of Boyd's quietly unhappy last years in Rome. I had thought of him as a rather tiresome character, amusing, but snobbish and a bit precious. I wouldn't have expected his life to yield much in the way of human interest—or for that matter, narrative interest. An unlived life, I might well have said, mistakenly. It was the final entries that I found moving. Living alone, very short of money, his last novel a failure, often very lonely, Boyd had to face his own death from cancer. He recorded his own frailty, measuring it every day by the number of steps he could take across the room, fewer and fewer each day. 'I grow weaker & weaker & can only hope to die soon', he wrote. Yet he could rouse himself to talk to visitors and make jokes about his condition and, as I later discovered, he was writing letters to friends in England and family in Australia which were funny, spirited and gossipy, with no hint of how desperate, financially and physically, his state had become.

I had never thought of Boyd as a battler. He had often presented himself, with due irony, as someone who would always find the softest cushion and sit on it, but when I read the diary entries of those last months the battler and stoic came to mind. It was from that point—contemplating the way Boyd faced his death—that I felt I wanted to know the beginnings; and as I went back to look at the whole life, including his service in the First World War, I knew there was a story to tell.

It was in many ways the ideal distance in time for a biography. Boyd was nearly seventy-nine when he died. His closest ties were his family: his sister, nephews and nieces. There was no keeper of the flame. Guy Boyd, the chosen heir and literary executor, did not show any anxiety about what I might write. If there had been lovers, no one seemed to know them; and to this day none has been plausibly claimed, though there has been plenty of speculation.

Would I be walking on ashes? It didn't seem likely, although the careful and experienced publisher, Peter Ryan, urged me to get written permission to use any material by Martin Boyd, published or unpublished, in which Guy Boyd as literary executor held copyright. I typed a letter, and took it to Guy, who signed it so instantly and trustfully that I felt guilty—what if I did find something? It's one of the hazards of biography that a close relationship with subject or copyright holder can bind the author as tightly as any legal agreement. The Boyd charm, and my sense, perhaps mistaken, of Guy Boyd's innocent compliance, would make me hesitate to use that legal weapon.

By the end of 1984 I was seriously at work on the Boyd biography. I had the great advantage of privileged access to the Boyd archive, collected for the National Library by bibliographer Terry O'Neill who had saved many Boyd letters from Melbourne bonfires as their ageing owners tidied up their houses. He had also made contact during some months in the UK with a number of Boyd's English friends, with whom he taped interviews for the National Library collection. Following in his footsteps, I had the good fortune of knowing what had been recorded, and what gaps I would want to fill in interviewing the same people. The ranks of Boyd's generation were thinning, but those who survived into their nineties were remarkably candid.

The most important interviews within Australia were those I recorded in Wagga Wagga with Martin Boyd's sister Helen Read. She talked the more freely because, as she said, so much nonsense was published about the next generation of Boyds: her nephews Arthur, Guy, David and Robin. There were matters she wanted to set straight about her own parents, Emma Minnie and Arthur Merric Boyd, whose memory she cherished. Because she was able to evoke her own childhood so vividly, I had a wonderfully fresh account of the family life Martin Boyd knew. Unsentimental, direct, with a sharp comic sense, Helen Read at eighty-two did not have her stories cut-and-dried through repetition. As we talked, with the tape recorder running, she was struggling to reach back into her childhood, and above all to get it right. Her memories of her brothers Penleigh and Martin were loving and untroubled. She was anxious to be fair to her eldest brother Merric, with whom she had belatedly come to sympathise when she discovered that he had epilepsy. In her childhood at the turn of the century, when epilepsy was still linked with insanity and criminal behaviour, Merric's disability was kept secret for good reason. Yet Helen Read found it hard to reconcile the absolute truthfulness, to which her mother by nature and religious belief was committed, with a cover-up that damaged relationships between the Boyd siblings.

Another candid witness of early years was Isla Marsh (née Chomley), first cousin to Martin, who was in her nineties when I met her at her son's house in Perth one hot afternoon in 1984. To her, 'young Marty' was still the fresh-faced boy who came to her parents' house in London in 1916 in his very new military uniform. Marty was a 'nice boy', but why, she asked accusingly, wasn't I writing about Penleigh instead? Penleigh was so gifted, so handsome, so charming. 'Now *that* would be a book.'

To prompt her memories, Isla Marsh brought out her diaries of the First World War, and read me some tantalising vignettes of Marty and Pen. Then, suddenly tired, she announced that she would have a rest. Leaving me alone with the diaries and some photograph albums, she disappeared for an hour or more, leaving a volume open on the dining table. I was tempted to continue reading for myself but didn't dare. Isla Marsh's beauty, seen in old photographs, remained in her large, dark eyes. I thought of the scene in *The Aspern Papers*, when the 'publishing scoundrel', caught like a burglar with the box of love letters, meets the glare of the 'extraordinary eyes' of Juliana, the long-dead poet's muse and mistress. A year or two later, after Isla Marsh's death, her diaries and other papers were given to the National Library where I read them with a clear conscience.

One of the best interviews about the young Martin Boyd was given by the improbably named Miss Pinkie de Long, who had worked with him in the Melbourne architectural firm of Purchas and Teague. She too remembered a 'nice boy', but had her doubts about his future as an architect: 'he couldn't be bothered with drains—that sort of thing'. More valuable was her memory of his decision, unwillingly taken, to volunteer for war service in 1915. The casualty lists from Gallipoli had just appeared; several friends had been killed and he felt he had to go. She even remembered the time and place of his decision: a National Gallery art students' fancy dress ball at which young Marty, as she called him, appeared as a leprechaun in a dark shirt with bright green spots painted on it from his mother's paintbox.

I had to wait for study leave in 1985 before interviewing Boyd's English friends. Travelling in his expatriate footsteps, from Melbourne to London and Sussex, the Lake District and Rome, it all went quite smoothly. His friends remembered him with affection; there were good stories to tell, and a sense of personality began to emerge. So far as I could tell, people talked very freely, rummaged around for old letters and handed them over with no conditions. But I remember one issue of conscience of the kind that Dr Johnson would understand. I was given a bundle of letters written by Boyd to some Cambridge friends. They were good letters: a testimony to his capacity for friendship. They were also performance pieces. Boyd told a good story and he could be malicious.

I had to face this aspect of his personality when in one of the Cambridge letters I found a very unkind account of a woman I had already met. She's dead now but she can stay anonymous, a Mrs X. It was perfectly obvious to me that Mrs X, a rather sad and lonely divorced woman, had been in love with Boyd. She showed me affectionate letters he had written to her which, with a slight reluctance that showed how much they meant to her, she let me take back to my hotel to read and return to her next day.

Now, what does the responsible biographer do in this situation? I had Guy Boyd's permission to quote anything Martin ever wrote. I didn't want to make Martin out to be a saint, and here was a prime example of his contradictory nature. He was a generous friend to Mrs X, for whom he took real trouble when she was ill and unhappy, and yet he ridiculed her for the sake of a funny story when writing to his Cambridge friends, who didn't know her and so didn't judge his disloyalty.

Of course I didn't quote the unkind story of Mrs X. I knew she would read my biography and recognise herself, and she would be devastated. Her love for Martin Boyd, misguided though it was, exemplified Dr Johnson's dilemma. This fire wasn't extinguished. My way out was made easier by the discovery of another letter, not quite as good, but of a similar kind, about another woman—and besides this woman was dead.

Time and distance, as the 'walking on ashes' metaphor suggests, have a habit of deciding things for the biographer. I discovered a family secret, which would have caused a great deal of trouble if Martin Boyd had been still living. His great-grandfather John Mills, who died in 1841, had been a convict, transported to serve seven years in Van Diemen's Land. That should not have been a problem so many years later but family secrecy about his existence brought complications.

The convict records revealed a quite startling story. Convicted of burglary and theft in 1826, John Mills, a Gloucestershire labourer, was given the light sentence of seven years because he was only sixteen at the time of his conviction. His whole family was active in a group known as the Wickwar Gang, which carried out robberies and thefts for some years before being rounded up. The Mills family fireplace was a repository for stolen goods of all kinds, including sides of bacon and a bag of half-crown coins. After the arrests, one brother turned King's Evidence, thereby saving himself, his parents and sisters. Another brother, twenty-seven-year-old William Mills, who had a long history of criminal activity, was hanged in Gloucester Gaol. His execution was followed by a shooting in which Unity Mills, the mother of the family, was wounded. The informer Thomas Mills had to leave the neighbourhood for fear of more reprisals.

No matter how much, in today's thinking, a convict ancestor has risen in acceptability, even gaining trophy status, I don't think many would relish the wholesale appropriation of other people's goods in the manner of the Mills family. And the hanging of William Mills casts a dark shadow. The story was fully documented in court proceedings, down to the judge's address to the jury, recommending the death penalty. Local history records included the testimony of the chaplain who prayed with Mills on the morning of his execution. In some circumstances, perhaps, I could simply have told the story of John Mills, but left it in the past—just a colourful anecdote which didn't really impinge on the lives of the twentieth-century descendants. But, as William Faulkner says: 'The past is not dead. It's not even past.'

John Mills was very much present as an influence on his descendants for nearly a century after his death, even though they never knew it. His story had to be told in my life of Martin Boyd, because it directly affected the way in which the Boyds grew up. It affected—indeed it created—the family style. Two generations of artists were sustained by the fortune made in early Melbourne by this unpromising young lawbreaker.

After serving his seven years in Van Diemen's Land, where he learned the brewing trade, John Mills came to Melbourne in 1837, bought land in what became the central business district, and established a brewery and several public houses. When he died in 1841, he left only one child. Three-year-old Emma Mills inherited valuable properties which, after the gold rushes and the consequent growth of Melbourne, made her immensely rich.

The next part of the story sounds like True Romance but it is fully documented in public records and private diaries. Emma Mills spent much of her childhood in her father's brewery under the erratic guardianship of her mother's second husband, the brewery foreman Thomas Robinson. Soon after Mills' death, Robinson began a long legal struggle to get possession of some of the child's inheritance; and as its value grew it was also assailed by two of Emma's uncles, Thomas and Job Mills, who came from England to make a claim on the estate. There were many Supreme Court hearings, presided over by that austere figure, Chief Justice William à Beckett. Robinson, a persistent litigant, spent months in gaol for contempt of court. Hannah Robinson left her husband and with Emma's half-brothers and sisters, went to live at Berwick. Emma was made a ward of the court so that her interests could be protected.

By all accounts Emma was pretty, charming and intelligent. She was given a young lady's education in Melbourne among the daughters of the colony's gentlefolk. Aged seventeen, she was courted by the impulsive Willie à Beckett, the Chief Justice's eldest son, who was then just twenty-one. They met in secret, and within a few months of his ardent declaration of love, Emma accepted Willie's proposal of marriage. For the à Becketts, it was deeply embarrassing. For this upper-class family, well connected in England, Emma's parentage could hardly have been worse. She would bring the convict stain into the family: unthinkably, there would be à Beckett children with convict blood. An honest labouring family would have been bad enough, but the Mills' collective history of crime must have appalled the à Becketts. John Mills, mercifully, was dead, but very much alive and present was Hannah Mills, now Hannah Robinson, to whom Emma was always a loyal and devoted daughter. Hannah wasn't from a convict family, but she lacked education, as I discovered when I saw her marriage certificate. She didn't sign it; she made her mark.

The young couple didn't elope. They had the quietest wedding imaginable in the little church of St Peter, East Melbourne, a short walk from the stately surroundings of Bishopscourt, which the à Becketts were renting from the Archbishop of Melbourne while they built themselves a new house. Two witnesses only: no embarrassing Robinsons, but no Sir William or Lady à Beckett either. Emma and Willie went to Geelong for a few days;

and, according to one of the à Beckett cousins, the first that she or anyone else heard of this astonishing alliance was a piece of wedding cake, wrapped in newspaper. It is to the credit of the à Beckett family that Emma's marriage settlement safeguarded her to the extent of having half her fortune come under her control from the age of twenty-one. That was not usual in those days: married women seldom had such freedom. It had far-reaching effects in her ability to do as she pleased when her marriage came under strain. She was free to choose a life in Australia when her husband would have liked to be a country squire in England.

The à Beckett family welcomed Emma, and as I read her diaries I had no doubt of the affection she won from them all. She was an exceptionally charming and lovable woman. It was hard for Sir William, not only because he was Chief Justice, but because he had for some years taken a very strong line in public against the liquor trade. He had described pubs as 'plague spots'—and here was his eldest son living on their proceeds. Sir William's new house in East Melbourne was completed, but he did not live there long. Pleading ill health, he resigned from the Supreme Court and returned to England, where he again became active in the Total Abstinence movement. Presumably the affronted gentlefolk of Melbourne stopped gossiping about the intruder's murky antecedents. Silence about the origins of the à Beckett money was interpreted in later years to mean no more than the shame of its coming from the liquor trade. Behind the brewery the convict stood, invisible.

As this story unrolled itself before my fascinated gaze, I was not sure how to deal with it so far as the living Boyds were concerned. Should I tell them first, or just write it, and see what happened? It had to be told, and there was no question of fencing it off from the main narrative of Emma Mills à Beckett's grandson Martin. As I read his account of his grandmother I felt sure that he had discovered her history and taken pains to suppress it. And the convict story was crucial as a shaping influence on his own life. There was a long straight line from Gloucester Gaol to penal servitude in Van Diemen's Land, to the Melbourne brewery and its satellite public houses, and to the idyllic pastoral childhood of the young Boyds at Sandringham on Port Phillip Bay and on their farm at Yarra Glen.

The diaries of Emma Mills à Beckett showed her passion for art, and her undeviating commitment to the artistic talent of her children. Her daughter Emma Minnie (known as Minnie) was the delight of Emma's life; and when her marriage to the feckless Willie à Beckett lost its lustre, she drew the greatest satisfaction from the painting career of Minnie, who married another painter, Arthur Merric Boyd, in 1886. Arthur had no money and no prospects, but he and Minnie were perfectly suited in temperament and their mutual devotion to a painting career. Sustained by an allowance from Emma, they never needed to worry about selling their work. Emma took them to Europe, looked after their children while they painted in France and Spain, and exulted when they both had works exhibited at the Royal Academy in London in 1891. Always their patron, Emma bought Boyd landscapes to give away as wedding presents; and to make sure that her daughter's Royal Academy triumph was known in Melbourne, she bought the painting and donated it to the National Gallery of Victoria.

Martin Boyd grew up in an atmosphere of carefree creativity, tempered by his mother's religious fundamentalism. Neither he nor his brothers, Merric the potter and Penleigh the landscape painter, ever took a regular paid job; and even when their inheritance from their grandmother's fortune dwindled to nothing, their sense of themselves as artists was immutable, thanks to the convict's money. This was something Martin Boyd never acknowledged. And his refusal to face it—his denial, in fact, that there was any ungentlemanly matter in his family history—was on record, again and again. He had made himself the family historian: he had drawn family trees and sought out remote ancestors for the Boyds and the à Becketts. But he never mentioned his great-grandfather Mills, except to say in passing that his city property had enriched his daughter Emma. In Martin's telling, Mills sounds much more like an investor than an ex-convict pub keeper and brewer. And there is not a word about the Gloucestershire family, with whom during his long expatriate years, Martin could have claimed kin.

I could see that Martin Boyd would have been appalled by the story I was about to tell. But would it matter to the next generation—in particular to Guy Boyd? I didn't think it would, but in one of my interviews I was warned that I would strike trouble. The warning came from writer Geoffrey Dutton, who in the early 1970s had embarked on a Boyd family history. He had Australia Council support, he had a research assistant and a contract with a London publisher, Secker and Warburg; and he had spent nearly a year on the project. 'You won't get them to co-operate', Dutton told me. The trouble, he said, would come from Guy and Phyllis Boyd, who, after initial friendliness had suddenly closed the door against him. I couldn't quite see how that settled the matter for Dutton. He had Arthur and David Boyd, and their sister Mary Perceval (later Mary Nolan) ready and willing. He had been to Rome and had been given, as he said ' the dying Martin's blessing'.[2] If Martin was happy to have Dutton write the family story, it seemed odd that Guy's opposition was so decisive. Dutton generously gave me his research notes, from which I could see that he knew about the convict but had not looked into the case history. At some stage, presumably, he would have done so, and there would be no chance of hiding the Wickwar Gang.

Years later, Dutton published an account of the project in which he said that the 'implacable opposition' to any form of family biography he had encountered from Guy and Phyllis Boyd had made his task impossible.[3] He blamed them completely—hence his warning that they might suddenly turn against my work, as they had turned against his. This was bad news, but I couldn't quite believe it. I pressed on, hoping that Dutton was wrong: and that, whatever the problem, time might have solved it.

If the problem was not the convict story, what was it? It could have been the question of Martin Boyd's presumed homosexuality. That question was not new; people had been speculating for years about it, and Boyd's novels as well as his two autobiographies gave it credence. Yet Guy Boyd's sudden turning against the Dutton book suggests that something happened in 1971 or early 1972, just before Martin's death. And that event—if I am right—was Arthur Boyd's chance encounter in Canberra in 1971 with the distant cousins from the Mills family who told the convict story. It was passed on to Dutton, and then to Martin in Rome—hence the explosion which made Dutton give up.

As I pressed on with my research, however, it was Martin Boyd's sexuality that most perplexed me. In interviews with his friends, the question often came to me: what did I think? Had I come across any love affairs? Some said that of course he was homosexual, and that there must have been lovers, but they couldn't name anyone. Others, like his old friend Max Nicholson, said that Martin never had the courage to commit himself: he would 'gaze at beautiful youths' but that was all. Nicholson, openly gay, rather despised Martin for his timidity. I talked to the King's College chorister, John Aldiss, whom the middle-aged Martin had invited to tea in the 1940s, and later taken on holidays to France. Aldiss, who was the model for Stephen in *Lucinda Brayford*, said that Martin was always 'very proper'. That was the note struck in all the interviews with the men, by now themselves middle-aged, who had known Martin in England when they were young. Perhaps there were affairs, they said, but 'not with me'. Is that what they would have said anyway? Perhaps; but I didn't sense any embarrassment, or lack of candour. An Anglican Franciscan friar, the Reverend Francis Tyndale-Biscoe, described Martin Boyd's attachment to him as 'sentimental'. No one spoke of passion.

Then there was the testimony of friends like Quinton Geering and his wife Jill who shared Boyd's Cambridge house for more than a year. 'Martin homosexual? Absolutely not. I would have known', Geering said. Jill Geering thought of him as 'asexual'. Sir Walter Crocker, Australian Ambassador to Italy during Boyd's years in Rome, agreed. Too fastidious for casual affairs, Crocker said, adding that he never heard any gossip about Boyd—and gossip about Australians in Italy usually reached the Embassy. The one strong attachment I had discerned from reading Boyd's Rome diaries and his autobiography *Day of My Delight* was with an Italian boy, Luciano Trombini.

With Trombini, sixteen when they met, to Boyd's fifty-seven, the relationship was variously described: father and son, teacher and pupil. Boyd never shared his house on equal terms with anyone, and even Trombini, who perhaps came closer than anyone else to an intimate everyday participation in Boyd's life, was no exception.

Yet Boyd was vulnerable to Trombini's moods. His carelessness, his inconsiderate comings and goings, provoked deep sadness as well as anger. And looking back, long after Trombini had married and moved away from Rome, Boyd wrote of this episode as 'the truest friendship of my life ... a happy time, an asset of memory'. I didn't interview Trombini. It wasn't easy to find him; my time in Rome was limited and my Italian language skills non-existent. For these reasons I turned for help to someone uniquely placed to search out Trombini and ask awkward questions. Desmond O'Grady, novelist, journalist and friend from our student days in Melbourne, has lived in Rome for many years, speaks perfect Italian, knew Boyd well. He could discern nuances and circumlocutions that would be lost in Trombini's English, which was not likely to be fluent. After I had returned to Australia, Desmond traced Trombini, took the train to Milan and talked to him on my behalf. The result was much the same as my own interviews in England. Trombini remembered Boyd as a wonderful teacher, a civilising influence, a generous friend. He was not embarrassed, not defensive in any way. It was evident that he had always thought of Boyd as an old man. A sexual relationship seemed most unlikely, O'Grady concluded.

Of course, that did not rule out sexual desire on Boyd's part; and as I re-read his novels I could see his own vision of self (or one of them—he was many-sided) in a series of elderly men, pathetic, sometimes absurd, in their yearning for a beautiful, indifferent youth. That,

I thought, was all I was likely to find; and I was relieved that there was nothing on the record likely to upset Guy Boyd. There was, however, one last-minute surprise. Sam Wood, an Australian who had known Boyd well in the late 1930s, showed me a recent letter from his cousin in England, Barbara Gill:

> re Martin Boyd's sex life ... I never was able to solve that mystery & I have recently made enquiries from an old friend aged 96 [Marjorie Michell[4]] who was his mistress for some years around Aunt Alice's [Alice Creswick's] time. Those many years ago it shook me to the roots when I discovered the situation—I had no idea he had it in him—like you I would have trusted him with anybody—but—I have consulted her and she does not think he was a 'homo' in spite of the way he behaved he gave one plenty of cause to suspect it.
>
> Marge is very bright mentally in spite of her great age ... she thinks it very unlikely Martin was ever more than a playboy in that direction—I don't suppose we will ever know the answer; so must give him the benefit of the doubt. Anyway he gave us all a good many laughs with his strange ways.[5]

This letter came too late for me to give it more than a hasty endnote. For me its value as testimony came from Barbara Gill's evident astonishment and by the dispassionate tone in which she and Marjorie Michell spoke about it so many years later. But because Sam Wood didn't think I should publish Marjorie Michell's name in her lifetime, my brief mention of the alleged affair seemed unconvincing to the few readers who noticed it. One critic, some years later, said that my failure to interview Luciano Trombini was part of a pattern of denial. He missed the point that by entrusting the interview to Desmond O'Grady I was sharing any possible revelations. It didn't occur to me to ask for confidentiality: Desmond was perfectly free to talk about the interview if he so wished. As it happened there was nothing to reveal, but I had no way of knowing that.

In 1988, when *Martin Boyd* was published, there was still a certain hesitation in discussing same-sex relationships. Writers of obituaries still used such phrases as 'confirmed bachelor'. David Marr's biography of Patrick White, which changed a great deal in the Australian literary scene, was not yet on the horizon; it would not appear until 1991. Leon Edel, re-reading his five-volume biography of Henry James for a one-volume abridgement, was startled to discover his own 'residual prairie puritanism':

> When I started rewriting certain passages I was suddenly aware of the extent to which the entire [sexual] revolution had liberated biography.[6]

His view of his subject had not changed, Edel said, but he was now free to write about 'the passional life of the celibate James … his homoerotic component, his transmuted passions, his latent prudery, his scrupulous avoidances and verbal barriers'.[7] Yet while Edel rejoiced in his new freedom, he suggested a quite different area in which reticence should be maintained. Although he was amused at the fact that in the 1950s he had been too prim to say that Henry James suffered from constipation, he attacked the biographer of Somerset Maugham for 'crossing the boundary of human dignity' in a detailed description of the novelist's old age of mental and bodily decay.

Edel would have disliked John Bayley's memoir of his wife Iris Murdoch, in which the novelist and philosopher appears as a dirty, dishevelled and incontinent victim of Alzheimer's disease, soothed by watching the Teletubbies. Yet the cases are not quite the same. Maugham's biography is distressing because of the tone of repugnance and distaste in which it is written. It is harder to judge Bayley's tone. He sees the portrait as a loving one, written with a sense of the continuity of Murdoch's life. Re-reading *Iris*, I wondered if the husband's love might not uneasily co-exist with a submerged hostility, an unacknowledged relish at seeing the brilliant Iris, the dominant partner in their marriage, so reduced? Impossible to be sure. As Michael Holroyd has said: 'The dead have never been able to control the living, nor the living the dead. What matters is the spirit in which they communicate, the imaginative link made between us and those who "though dead yet speaketh".'[8]

Anyone who spends the time and thought demanded by a full-length biography must develop a relationship with the subject. Sometimes it begins in idolatry and ends in disillusionment, even dislike. The whole range of human relationships is here, in distilled form, with irritation and boredom, as well as affection and amusement, as part of the biographical transaction. Protectiveness for Martin Boyd's reserve probably had its effect on my discussion of his sexuality. And if Edel was writing 'pre-revolutionary stuff', so was I. Nevertheless, my comment that Boyd 'repressed and aestheticised his sexuality' still seems right. Except for the surprise disclosure about Marjorie Michell, there was no evidence of any physical relationship to which a responsible biographer could refer. If I were to re-write *Martin Boyd* as Edel re-wrote his *Henry James,* I would say more about the complexities of the question, as I was able to do, within the limits of Martin's diminished role as one Boyd among many, in my group study, *The Boyds.* But in 1988 it seemed to me that I had told my readers all I knew, leaving them with as much insight as Boyd's closest friends, with their years of observation and guesswork, had possessed.

My interviews with Boyd's family members and his friends in Australia and England showed me his chameleon quality. The protective colouring he brought to each new setting made him hard to know; so did his habit of keeping his friends in separate compartments. With the intellectuals and bohemians of his Sussex years, he seemed relaxed and open-minded, not shocked by Jazz Age frivolity, ready for talk of Freud, free love and vegetarianism. A decade later, in rural Cambridgeshire, where he owned a few acres of farmland, with attendant sheep, he wore good tweeds, which did not make the mistake of looking new, and met local squire or rural labourer as if to the manor born. Yet, as he himself said, he 'never quite belonged'. English friends spoke of his 'breezy Australian informality' while there were many in Australia who thought he had become 'very English'. Role-playing came easily to Martin Boyd, and it is a safe conjecture that it concealed an inner loneliness. No wonder that friends disagreed so sharply about his sex life; they saw such divergent selves. Virginia Woolf believed that a biographer could expect to capture no more than six or seven of our multiple selves. If I found four or five Martin Boyds—and I think I did—I would be satisfied, but looking back I believe that I could have written more searchingly about his elusiveness.

One problem for biographers is that we know the ending, though we may not know how to write it. Because my introduction to Martin Boyd came to me through his late diaries, those last images of exile and solitude in his sad but indomitable old age had their influence in my reading of the early life, in which I discerned images of homelessness. Consciously or not, I was shaping a narrative for which his death in Rome was the inevitable conclusion. Virginia Woolf's biographer, Hermione Lee, discussing the ways we can choose to write the end of a life, speaks of the author's need to find meaning there:

> … biographical readings of their subject's end in which a gesture, a last word or a final act are given

> value and significance, or in which the subject's work is invoked at the moment of death, sustain the old tradition of the deathbed scene that concludes the meaning of the life; but this may be quite incongruous for our post-Freudian, post-Beckettian, times. Yet it is still very unusual for death in biography to occur as random, disorderly, without meaning, without relation to the life lived and without conclusiveness.[10]

Was my portrait of Boyd given its tone of regret by the awareness of how little, in the end, would remain to be weighed in his mind against his sense of failure as a writer and in his personal relationships? Inevitably, I think it was. And, like all biographies, it was limited by the material available to me. The perceptions of living witnesses vary, and I would like to think that I can use them discerningly, but they are always limited in number, their memories random, sometimes unreliable.

My portrait of Boyd was made up of dots of colour, *pointilliste* style, from various interviews in England and Australia. In the mid-1980s it was too late to find any of the few survivors of his Royal Flying Corps days. Some women in their nineties remembered 'young Marty Boyd', but apart from a letter to a fellow officer signed 'Toodle-pip', there was no direct testimony of the way he had presented himself during war service. His 'qualified pacifism' seems not to have emerged for many years—perhaps not until the political climate of the 1930s forced him to confront his war experience, as he did, first in autobiography and much later in fiction.

Biography does the best it can with an uneven spread of evidence. I had the testimony of a sister and several cousins, three nephews, dozens of friends. His grandmother's diaries gave glimpses of the young child; his headmaster's daughters remembered the schoolboy. As biographies go, it was well documented, but like most biographies it had large gaps and uncertainties. I didn't build myself in as narrator to comment on the gaps, nor did I describe the tracks I covered, except in the endnotes which documented the interviews.

Some moments linger in memory. An awkward pause at lunch with one of the older à Beckett cousins. 'You know, there's no convict blood in our family', she said confidently. I had not long before read the diary of the chaplain who attended her great-great-uncle William Mills before his execution in Gloucester Gaol; and the whole story of the Wickwar Gang was vividly present to me as I listened to a highly romanticised version of her grandparents' courtship which featured a runaway horse and a Government House ball. Should I have put down my soup spoon to say: 'It wasn't like that'? Moral cowardice and the duty of a guest kept me silent.

A good memory: Arthur Boyd's generosity when we first met, at his house on the Shoalhaven. I didn't find him easy to interview. My questions about Uncle Martin fell into long silences. In an effort to be absolutely truthful, Arthur tended to qualify his statements, so that a promising idea would slide away, and I would be left, pencil in mid-air, with nothing to write. Whether Arthur thought the biography was misguided, or whether he found my questions dull, I wasn't sure. I thought once more of Geoffrey Dutton's warning that the Boyd family would never co-operate. But once I had closed my notebook, feeling a failure, Arthur became anxiously helpful. Was there anything I wanted to see? What else could he do to help? Gesturing vaguely at his own paintings in the Bundanon drawing room, he asked: 'Are you interested in this sort of thing?' and added hastily 'I wouldn't be, if I were you'. It was time to go and I thought Arthur had had enough. But he came to the car, wished me well with the book, and added: 'If you want a quiet place to write it, you can always come here'. His daughter Polly added later: 'Dad meant it; you could come here if you liked'.

Among those I interviewed, I didn't find anyone who strongly disliked Martin Boyd, and in England he was remembered with warmth and affection. In Australia, there were some dissonant voices. As an expatriate ('very English, rather patronising') he was seen by some to have let down the side. Neighbours at Harkaway, where he renovated his à Beckett grandfather's house during his brief return in the late 1940s, described him as 'a bit of a duffer'. Tradesmen 'saw him coming'; he hadn't enough sense to check their work and it was no wonder the roof leaked—anyone else would have climbed up to have a look before writing the cheque. This matched the story told by Cambridgeshire neighbours. Having authorised an agent to buy some sheep for his few acres of land, Martin became so excited that he started bidding against himself, and so became the owner of the most expensive sheep in the county.

Within the à Beckett–Boyd family there were some who remembered angrily the way he had pillaged family history in *The Montforts* (1928) and in the Langton tetralogy (1952–63). They had good reason. Boyd's habit of fusing the stories of two or more family members and adding some fictional elements—usually disreputable—was especially provocative. Boyd had put up the unconvincing defence that, because he was a long way from Melbourne when he wrote these novels, he had thought that his aunts and cousins 'wouldn't mind'. They did mind; and although in later years the precise grounds for outrage were half forgotten, the grievance still smouldered and I sometimes felt I should apologise on his behalf. Martin Boyd's priorities were revealing. While he endowed his à Beckett grandfather with a mistress and four illegitimate sons, he protected his grandmother, the convict's daughter, with a wholly fictitious background among the gentry.

With the convict story told in detail I went on with the biography, wondering now and then how Guy Boyd would take it. He and his family moved to Canada soon after I started work on the book, and by the time they returned to live permanently in Australia, I had almost finished. With some trepidation I asked Guy if he would like to read the book. Ominously, he said that he would. 'You know, if there's anything to upset the family, they'll all blame me.' I suggested that, if he didn't read it, he would be in the clear. 'Then they can blame the author.' This ploy failed. Gently, inexorably, Guy said, 'No, I think it's my duty to read it'.

I timed the delivery of the manuscript to reach Guy just as I left for Canberra where, during a short stay at the Humanities Research Centre, I checked quotations from the Boyd and à Beckett papers in the National Library. I didn't give Guy a phone number, reasoning that if initially he was shocked by the convict story or anything else, he would have had time to calm down. His friendliness at our last meeting was so obviously unfeigned that I couldn't believe there would be any trouble. And yet I couldn't forget Geoffrey Dutton's warning that he could change overnight, and torpedo my publication. Of course I was armed with Guy's letter, giving copyright permission, but my liking for Guy and Phyllis, as well as the other Boyds, had grown so much that any breach would have been distressing.

I had been in Canberra only two or three days when I was called to the phone at the Humanities Research Centre. Somehow, Guy had tracked me down. His first words were reassuring. He had been sitting up half the night to finish the biography, and he thought it was wonderful. And with a slightly ambiguous compliment, he gave the final accolade: 'I never thought that Uncle Martin's life could be made so interesting!'

So all my anxieties were needless. Guy Boyd's attitude to my biography was consistently encouraging and helpful. What then to make of Dutton's experience? Had time resolved a problem and if so, what was it? Dutton never knew the reason. His autobiography, *Out in the Open* (2002), records a lasting puzzle and a deep grievance. Guy Boyd died suddenly just before my book was published. I hadn't asked him about the Dutton book, and because all the Boyds seemed happy about what I had written—including the convict story—it no longer seemed important.

Just two years ago I had the hint of an explanation in a casual remark from David Boyd, recalling a letter from Martin to Guy after the Dutton visit to Rome. For all Martin's frailty in those last weeks of his life, he had strength enough to exert authority over his nephew and heir. Dutton had to be stopped, he told Guy. If the convict story came out 'I would be ruined'. Guy could not give Dutton the real reason; and it's easy to see why. Martin's family research was thorough, even obsessive: he must have known the Mills story, and with its revelation it would be evident to the world that his own gentlemanly pretensions were false. Among the upper-class friends of his years in England Martin had often heard the little convict jokes at his expense: 'Boyd is an Australian but I still have all my spoons' was one of them. Social shame seems likely as the prime motive. As well as that, he put a high value on truthfulness. And if he hadn't lied about his ancestry he had certainly been thrifty with the truth. Some lofty pronouncements would have come back to haunt him. So, faced with an urgent plea from a dying man, Guy would have given his promise, and even after

Martin's death soon afterwards, would have felt bound to hold his position.

If this explanation is the right one, what had changed by 1985, when I came along? What made Guy Boyd so happily sign away his copyright permissions to me? I can only think that with the lapse of time he no longer felt that Martin's wishes could—or should—be protected. By then the secret was out; the convict story had been told by David Boyd in the *Bulletin* in 1980, although in a sentimentalised version in which Mills was the victim of a mistaken arrest.[11] So it seems most likely that Martin Boyd was given the reassurance he wanted before he died and that particular hot coal in the Boyd story died down to ashes.

7

Searching for the Subject: Georgiana McCrae

Only connect, E.M. Forster reminds us. For biographers, the first connections between subject and author may be a single image, a poem, even a phrase, which sets the imagination working. For my biography of Georgiana McCrae, the first impulse came from a place where I could imagine this reluctant pioneer. There at Arthur's Seat, near Dromana, on the Mornington Peninsula, was the homestead built to Georgiana's design in 1845. There she walked on the beach with her children, deftly killed a snake with her parasol, sketched the unfamiliar eucalypts, planted English roses in her garden, made friends with members of the Bunurong tribe and tried to learn their language. This was the landscape that, much changed by time, I knew from summer holidays at Mount Martha, and visits to friends at Dromana.

In my childhood, well before freeways speeded the journey, we were impatient at what seemed a long drive down Point Nepean Road, counting the names of semi-suburban bayside places. Please Slow Down signs announced Mordialloc, Aspendale, Edithvale, Carrum, Seaford, Frankston. Not until we passed Mount Eliza was there a sense of uninterrupted space, farmland, dense tea-tree. Mount Martha, in the 1930s and early 1940s, was semi-rural. The one store, Ferraro's, had the only petrol pump; and on its crowded, unpredictable shelves, you might find calamine lotion for sunburn beside the tins of baked beans or packets of nails and picture wire. Ferraro's doubled as the Post Office; and on the way home from the beach we could collect the mail and sit on the wooden steps, barefoot, sand between the toes, eating a penny icecream cone, before walking a little way up the hill to our rented house in Prescott Avenue. The roads that led off Point Nepean Road were dirt tracks, in my first memory, but when the war brought American army trainees to Balcombe Camp, in 1943 or 1944, it also brought high-quality macadamised surfaces to Dominion Road and others in the camp area. From semi-rural retreat to summer playground, and on towards affluent suburbia, Mount Martha and the whole Port Phillip Bay area changed fast. As a child, I imagined 'our' Mount Martha, and the whole Mornington Peninsula to be in its proper, original state when we first spent summer holidays there in the 1930s: a timeless place, with no history.

Not so, of course. Almost a century earlier, in 1845, Georgiana and Andrew McCrae travelled by sea from Melbourne to a newly established cattle run at Arthur's Seat, bringing two small daughters, and a vast amount of household furniture to be unloaded on the beach. This place was home and fishing ground to the Bunurong people in whose long history the McCraes were intruders. Yet in a rare example of cultural accommodation the Bunurong would become the McCraes' friends. There, in moonlight on a stormy June night stands Georgiana in her full-skirted Victorian travelling dress, cape, bonnet and stout walking boots. A lantern shows the way through the scrub to her unfinished house, where her four young sons and their tutor are waiting.

That image, drawn from Georgiana's journal account of arrival at Arthur's Seat, came to mind when I first thought of writing her biography. It offered the connection between the known and the unknown which for me is crucial to the choice of subject. A region can be more than a physical background: a house can be more than a means of illustrating a way of life. With *Martin Boyd* there had been many images of place that gave me a sense of connection. His boarding school, Trinity Grammar, in Kew, was one. Another was his à Beckett grandparents' house in Church Street, Brighton. Just across the road from its turreted and gargoyled splendour was my grandparents' unremarkable 1920s villa. These and other images of place gave me access to Martin Boyd's early years. The dominant image of the biography was that of the old man adrift in Rome, but because of shared places in Melbourne, I knew how far he had drifted. With Georgiana, it was the same imaginative process, but in reverse order. I saw her at a point of arrival, on the beach at Arthur's Seat. Where she came from I had yet to discover.

The image of Georgiana on the beach, with the wish to write her story, wasn't a sudden illumination. For more than a year I'd been searching for a new subject. *Martin Boyd* succeeded beyond expectations, with good reviews, a quick reprinting followed by a paperback, two literary awards and many shortlistings. I wanted to do another biography, but no other subject came to mind. Friends made suggestions. We need a new life of Henry Lawson, someone said. That was beyond me: too big a gap. I didn't know Lawson's outback male world, nor the sad ending of Sydney streets, gaols, debts, alcoholic destitution. What about Kathleen Fitzpatrick, the historian whose brilliant lectures I remembered from my student days? Another convent-educated academic, who had written on Martin Boyd and Henry James—surely I could get close to her? The trouble with that idea was that it seemed too close. Exploring another Melbourne Catholic middle-class life didn't offer enough in the way of discovery. Besides, Fitzpatrick's memoir, *Solid Bluestone Foundations* (1983), was recent and enviably well written. Not only would

I be in danger of repetition, her work would write mine off the page.

I thought about other possibilities. In the 1980s the women's movement was reclaiming some neglected Australian women writers. Nettie Palmer came to mind, as someone who got scanty thanks for a lifetime in promoting other writers, including her novelist husband Vance Palmer. I spent a week or so at the National Library, Canberra, dipping into the Palmer papers. Somehow I couldn't feel any excitement there, and the handwriting was dauntingly difficult. Busy, hard-working Nettie Palmer deserved recognition, but I couldn't imagine spending three or four years in her company. A study of the Palmer marriage perhaps? I liked the idea of a double focus. But Palmer's novels—there were so many of them, and all of them dull. One day, in the Manuscripts Room at the National Library, Manning Clark leaned across the table to say, 'I must tell you, Brenda. I am in love with Nettie Palmer.' I don't know which of her papers prompted this announcement—perhaps her plaintive love letters to an indifferent Vance. I wasn't converted, but I kept Palmer in mind for a group study of several Australian women writers with parallel or intersecting careers. That idea, too, lapsed, because I could never see Palmer except in the sepia tones of a faded photograph.

If Palmer was penny plain, then Barbara Baynton was twopence coloured. In writing *Martin Boyd*, I had been intrigued by the expatriate Baynton, in whose flamboyant London life Boyd was briefly and embarrassingly entangled. When her third husband, the Viscount Headley, disappointed by her refusal to put money into his debt-laden estates, sued her for divorce, Boyd went into hiding, fearful of being named—however improbably—as co-respondent. Baynton interested me because of the huge gap between the fantasies of her social-climbing London life, based on a reinvention of her past, and the brutal realism of her short stories, set in the Australian outback. What would prompt her so brazenly to deny her working-class parentage, invent a new father, and live an outrageous lie? Martin Boyd's cousins gave entertaining accounts of 'Bayntie's' invasions of their house in London—always asking first what was for dinner—her extravagant clothes, her outsize jewels, her grand manner, and her redeeming comic sense. There were two main reasons to reject a Baynton biography. The major biographical discoveries about Baynton had been made by other scholars; and although my Boyd work added to the record, it was their territory. And, as with Nettie Palmer, though for different reasons, I didn't feel much empathy. I wrote an article on Baynton, and left it at that.

I looked at other possible subjects, none of them just right, until a chance meeting with historian Geoffrey Serle at a National Gallery party brought Georgiana McCrae into focus. As the author of *The Golden Age*, Serle was an authority on McCrae's period. His massive biography of John Monash had appeared in 1982 and when we talked at the National Gallery he was already at work on a life of Robin Boyd. Through his close association with the La Trobe Library he had taken an interest in the recent gift of the McCrae Family Papers, which had scarcely been used. Having read *Martin Boyd*, he thought that Georgiana McCrae would suit me. After the Gallery party, excited by the idea and the prospect of a rich family archive, I sat up late re-reading *Georgiana's Journals*, edited by Hugh McCrae in 1934. This time there was no mistake, but I let a day go by before telephoning Geoffrey Serle, in case he thought me too impetuous. He was quietly pleased to have made such a good match.

The scene had changed greatly in Australian biography since my New Haven hesitations of the 1970s. Serle's *Monash* was one important landmark. Another, whose psychological sophistication and elegant prose appealed to me, was John Rickard's *H.B. Higgins: the Rebel as Judge* (1987). Both Serle and Rickard were in the Monash History Department. Literary biography, as Geoffrey Serle remarked in 1979, was 'usually critical reviews … with a biographical sketch tacked on'. Looking back in 1992, in an important survey of the field, James Walter quoted Serle and pointed to Axel Clark's *Christopher Brennan* (1980) as one of the first in which life and work were integrated.[1] In 1987, a year ahead of *Martin Boyd*, Philip Ayres, an eighteenth-century scholar in the Monash English Department, published a life of Malcolm Fraser. This must have been seen as bordercrossing by those in the Politics Department; and by other literary scholars as an eccentric choice. Undeterred, Philip went on to write substantial scholarly biographies of Douglas Mawson, Owen Dixon and (his work in progress) Cardinal Moran. The appointment of Clive Probyn to the second chair of English at Monash in 1982 was another boost for biographical studies. *The Sociable Humanist*, Probyn's life of James Harris, was published in London in 1991, and his other research included substantial biographical work on Swift and Sarah Fielding. And as I began to think about Georgiana McCrae, Harold Love was working on his biography of James Edward Neild, a many-faceted man of letters in nineteenth-century Melbourne. Two important works by literary scholars in Adelaide and Sydney were Brian Matthews' *Louisa* (1987) and Drusilla Modjeska's *Poppy* (1994), which tested the boundaries with postmodern experiments in biographical form and asked crucial questions about the relationship between author and subject. Both *Louisa* and *Poppy* caught the imagination of a readership well beyond the academy.

Bordercrossing, work on the edge: biography was not quite sure of its place in literary studies. Although I was invited to talk to the Monash historians' research seminar, I would have been surprised to have a similar invitation from any department of English. Neither the 1985 expanded edition of the *Oxford Companion to Australian Literature*, nor its 1994 reprint, gives biography anything like the status of poetry, drama or fiction, where a very slim volume often wins its author a place. Axel Clark's name can be found in the Christopher Brennan and Henry Handel Richardson entries, but not under Clark.

My name gets in under Turner, Bruce and Boyd. And yet Axel Clark's *Christopher Brennan* and my *Martin Boyd* won literary prizes. What were we writing if it wasn't literature? My ration of comments and queries, after Boyd and later biographies appeared, often came addressed to me at the Department of History. Was that where I belonged? At any rate, the support and prestige of Geoffrey Serle effectively smoothed the way towards a life of Georgiana McCrae. Painter, diarist, pioneer, she could have been claimed by scholars in history or visual arts as well as literature.

Family approval would be the key, Geoffrey Serle said, offering an introduction to Miss Helen McCrae, who happened to be one of his neighbours in Lisson Grove, Hawthorn, as well as an old friend. I couldn't have had a better introduction. Helen McCrae's doubts about a biography of her great-grandmother melted away. If Dr Serle thought I was the right one, then the book would be 'in safe hands'. I didn't then know that safe hands might be needed. There was nothing in *Georgiana's Journals* to suggest family secrets. Over a series of talks with Helen McCrae, I discovered that, while the story was more complicated than that of the *Journals*, it was also a great deal more interesting. Behind the pioneering narrative was the romantic story of a Duke's daughter, illegitimate but acknowledged by the ducal family, brought up in Regency London among French émigré artists, beautiful, intelligent, talented and ambitious. After early success, frustrated in her dream of an artist's life, forbidden to marry the man she loved, Georgiana made her choice. She married Andrew McCrae, whose chequered fortunes eventually led to emigration and life in Australia.

A century after Georgiana's death her descendants were ready to have her story told. It hadn't always been so. When Marnie Bassett, author of *The Governor's Lady* (1940), a life of the wife of Philip Gidley King, wanted to write Georgiana's story, she was politely rebuffed. Hugh McCrae, who held most of the McCrae papers, reassured his anxious sister that he would 'fend off the old bird'. Bassett gave up and wrote *The Hentys* (1954) instead. It was a curious situation for the McCraes. Georgiana's illegitimate birth, the family secret, was a cause of pride as well as shame. Many family members would have liked to claim their direct descent from the last Duke of Gordon, but they couldn't do so without admitting the fact that he had not married Georgiana's mother. Georgiana had spoken and written openly about her parentage. Her papers reveal close ties with her father and grandfather, and her happy years at Gordon Castle. Jealousy on the part of her father's wife, who was childless, led to expulsion from the castle, marriage to Andrew McCrae and exile to Port Phillip in 1841.

One aspect of Georgiana's story was well known. In 1934 Hugh McCrae edited her Australian journals as part of Victoria's centenary celebrations. Georgiana was an early settler; she was also a witness of the historic moment in November 1850 when Victoria became an independent colony by an act of separation from New South Wales. Reprinted in 1965, the *Journals* were widely read. Historians greeted them as a rare, first-hand account of colonial settlement, vivid, witty and immediate. The McCraes were staying at Jolimont with Charles La Trobe and his wife Sophie on the day when La Trobe, formerly Superintendent of the Port Phillip District, became Governor of Victoria. Georgiana even took Sophie La Trobe's place in the ceremonial opening of the new bridge across the Yarra River. This episode was told with considerable verve in the published journals, as a high point in Georgiana's story. Even more appealing to women readers at least was her day-to-day account of pioneering struggles, as the mother of eight, wife to an apparently feckless, grumpy Andrew McCrae, whose financial ineptness caused the loss of two well-loved homes, first in Melbourne, later at Arthur's Seat.

This was the Georgiana I knew; and when I re-read the *Journals* I was responding to her first person voice, and her presence in the Mornington Peninsula region. I looked forward to exploring her background in England and Scotland, and to discovering how and where she had lived after the family left Arthur's Seat. A quick look through the McCrae Papers at the La Trobe Library was an exhilarating start. But first I wanted to meet the family in Sydney, whose co-operation would be essential. The copyright holders were Hugh McCrae's three granddaughters, with the eldest, Janet Hay, effectively in charge. When I visited Janet Hay and her husband Bill at Newport, the prospects of co-operation were all I had hoped for. Giving me the addresses of family members, Janet Hay alerted me to sensitivities, as well as to possible finds. Although the main family archive was in the La Trobe Library, some letters and notebooks were still privately held, as were some of Georgiana's paintings.

A few of the older members of the family, Janet said, disliked the word 'illegitimate'. They preferred to say that Georgiana was the Duke of Gordon's 'natural' daughter. This is the term Jane Austen uses in *Emma*, and it does sound gentler, less judgemental. Yet Georgiana herself did not hesitate to refer to one of her Gordon uncles as illegitimate.

With a contract from Melbourne University Press and an Australian Research Council grant to fund travel and research assistance, everything fell into place. At first MUP's director, John Iremonger, who had succeeded Peter Ryan in 1988, was reluctant to publish *Georgiana*. Colonial biographies didn't sell, he said; and because the McCrae *Journals* were still in print there might be no place for a new study. Iremonger's Sydney background didn't help. He underestimated Georgiana's status in Victoria as a pioneering heroine. However, persuaded by MUP's senior editor, Wendy Sutherland, Iremonger gave in; and the contract was signed. Someone said: 'Georgiana McCrae? That should be easy. You've got the *Journals*.' That wasn't my view. I needed the whole life, before and after the years of the *Journals*. But I did think the *Journals* would be central, and that because they were already in print, it would not be a huge task to check the originals for the inevitable variants or mistranscriptions. I was mistaken. The relationship between journals and manuscripts was complicated beyond belief.

The manuscripts, with which Hugh McCrae had worked to produce his 1934 edition, were not intact. The La Trobe Library, State Library of Victoria, held the first years of Georgiana's colonial experience, 1838–42, along with the other papers of the McCrae gift. The Fisher Library at the University of Sydney had the later years, from 1843 onwards. These included Georgiana's time at Arthur's Seat, and her account of the day on which Port Phillip became a state, independent of New South Wales. Hugh McCrae was responsible for this odd division. Keeping the first part of his grandmother's manuscript journal, he sold the remaining part to a collector, Harry S. Chaplin, from whom they eventually went to the Fisher Library.

As soon as I looked at the Fisher Library manuscripts, I knew something was wrong. I hadn't allowed time in Sydney for a detailed scrutiny, but even without placing the published text side by side with the manuscript, I noticed unexpected differences. New material was welcome, and not surprising; I looked forward to seeing what there was in the original that Hugh McCrae had cut out. Editors of his period weren't dedicated to precise reproduction—and McCrae was a poet, not a scholar. More disturbing was my sense of things missing which I'd read in *Georgiana's Journals*. If they weren't here, in Georgiana's handwriting, where did McCrae find them? It didn't then occur to me that he could have been reinventing his grandmother, still less that his embellishments could be pervasive.

There were some changes in the text for which I thought there might be sound reasons. As the diarist's grandson, Hugh McCrae could have heard family stories. It would be a liberty to put these into his grandmother's voice, but they might still be true. There was textual evidence that these manuscripts were not Georgiana's first day-to-day writings. In old age she made a fair copy of her earlier writings. Was it possible that Hugh McCrae, who was thirteen when his grandmother died, had a chance to read the originals? Assuming she destroyed them, as was her habit, how much could Hugh have remembered, more than forty years later? The more closely I looked, the more clearly I could see that to rely on Hugh McCrae's text would get me into deep trouble.

I wasn't the first to puzzle over Hugh McCrae's interventions. In her final honours thesis for the Monash History Department in 1980 Marguerite Hancock, who found the same discrepancies, worked from the manuscript version, in Georgiana's undeniable handwriting. I made the same decision. I decided to forget Hugh McCrae's text and find 'my' Georgiana in her manuscript, and in whatever other sources could be found in public records and family papers. Meanwhile, my research grant would pay for the production of a reliable text from microfilms that I ordered from the two libraries. Not only would Georgiana's every word be transcribed, this version would give her spelling and punctuation—sometimes erratic—due attention. While this task was being carried out with scholarly precision by an experienced research assistant, Meredith Sherlock, I turned to other sources.

Material for a biography never comes in orderly progression. It can be planned in cradle-to-grave sequence, but even before I looked for the young Georgiana, starting with her baptismal certificate, I read some letters, written in her old age, which had a strong influence. Nothing in the Hugh McCrae text, which affirms the pioneer survivor, had prepared me for the desolation Georgiana expressed as she looked back to her early years in London and Scotland, and the painter's life she had left behind. In January 1887 the Portuguese artist Arthur Loureiro, then working in Melbourne, asked permission to paint a portrait of Georgiana, to whom he introduced himself as her 'brother brush'. The occasion opened the gates to memory. At eighty-three, after more than half a lifetime in exile, as she called her Australian years, Georgiana mourned her ambitious sixteen-year-old self. On her first public appearance, before the Duke of Sussex and a large audience she accepted a silver palette, a major prize for a painting by a promising young artist. Recalling that day, Georgiana put aside her mask of stoicism:

> What a happy woman I should have been had I but been allowed to continue the practice of my

> profession! To say nothing of the competency I might have amassed. But in those 'stuck-up' days it was considered *infra dig* for the wife of a gentleman to exhibit her talents for pecuniary recompense. The world is wiser nowadays—& talents no longer kept down under bushels but freely employed—as their Giver intended they should be—for the good & enjoyment of one's fellow creatures—Ach, my dear, too late for your ambitious old grannie! However it is soothing to have one's abilities recognised by a celebrity [Loureiro] in the Antipodes.[2]

Georgiana's letter was unexpected in its sense of alienation and unfulfilled destiny. This wasn't a contented matriarch. She had founded a family and played a part in the cultural life of the colony, but she felt no sense of achievement. 'I find that I have spent more than half of my lifetime in this *fifty-year-old town*', she wrote, disdainfully underscoring her words. Yet this was Marvellous Melbourne's Jubilee year. With her words in mind I looked at the Loureiro portrait, and thought that he had captured her sadness as well as her humour and energy. It was not a study of serene old age. Between them, the letter and the portrait displaced my first image of Georgiana, on the beach at Arthur's Seat. There and then I decided to begin the story at this moment, with Georgiana's backward glance at her unlived life as an artist. It was my dominant image in 1993 when I set out for London and Scotland.

Fragments of autobiography in the McCrae Papers gave evidence of Georgiana's unusual upbringing in Regency London. Her training as a professional portrait painter marked her out as an exception. Other young women of her time learned painting as one of the accomplishments expected in the marriage market, but not as professionals. A painter's career, marginally more respectable for a woman than life on the stage, demanded qualities of independence, self-reliance and competitiveness that were alien to the period's concept of womanhood. A writer could publish anonymously, as Fanny Burney and Jane Austen had done or, like the Brontës, choose a male pseudonym. A portrait painter had to meet her sitters face to face. Samuel Johnson had summed it up. 'Portrait painting is an improper employment for a woman. Publick practice of any art and staring in men's faces is very indelicate in a female.'[3] Her own account of childhood and early education didn't explain Georgiana's being allowed—even encouraged—to enter the professional artists' world. Her parentage, I thought, must hold the key to the mystery.

Dukes are highly visible people; their mistresses are not. I found contemporary accounts of Georgiana's father, George, fifth Duke of Gordon, and his father, Alexander. I hoped that the Gordon papers would bring Georgiana's mother, Jane Graham, from the shadows, if only as a charge on the ducal estate. But first, to look for her in London. One important piece of evidence was Georgiana's baptismal record, found in the fashionable

St James' Church, Piccadilly. I matched this exciting discovery by taking a photograph of the elegant baptismal font, carved by Grinling Gibbons, as a reminder that, although born out of wedlock, this child came into the world without apology. George, Marquis of Huntly, her father, signed the register in public acknowledgement of his daughter. Under Mother's Name, Jane Graham appeared. No sign of the clandestine marriage in which some of Georgiana's descendants invested romantic hopes. In a day's work on the rate books in the local history collection at the Swiss Cottage Library, I had a moment of triumph when Jane Graham's name duly appeared, confirming Georgiana's account of their years in shabby bohemian Somers Town. Apart from Jane Graham's death certificate, confirming that she never married, I could find nothing else about her. Her portrait by an unknown artist, held by a McCrae descendant, only compounds the mystery.

The Gordon papers, some held in the austerely beautiful classical surroundings of Register House, Edinburgh, and others in the West Sussex record office of the cathedral town of Chichester, repaid my searches, though inevitably some gaps remained. The Dukes of Gordon acknowledged their illegitimate children, loved them (sometimes more than their legitimate offspring), educated them, gave them the Gordon name, and provided handsome dowries. Here was Georgiana's half-sister, Susan Gordon, and half-brother Charles (later Admiral Gordon), both born in Scotland to Ann Thomson.

Georgiana had told the truth about her Gordon origins, no matter how much her story sounded like romantic fiction.

I would have liked to finish my travels in Scotland with a glimpse of the picture gallery at Gordon Castle, where Georgiana had copied paintings from her grandfather's collection. The wife of the present owner, however, wasn't interested in an Australian writer's search for a long-dead Gordon. 'I fear I am not well enough to receive you', she said unconvincingly on the telephone, adding in the authentic tone of a Lady Catherine de Bourgh, 'You would be welcome to walk in the grounds'. So with that qualified welcome, I walked one summer afternoon in the paths where, until an envious stepmother contrived her banishment, the young Georgiana Gordon had walked and sketched. Looking up from the neglected rose garden at Gordon Castle's magnificent heights I measured in memory the small room—hardly a cupboard in comparison—at Arthur's Seat from which Georgiana gazed out to sea.

It was an exhilarating though sometimes frustrating summer. Outdoors or indoors, studying portraits in galleries, exploring Highland castles and the streetscapes of Edinburgh's Old Town, or taking notes in record offices, I couldn't have drawn the line between work and pleasure. Gordon Castle, Morayshire, in north-east Scotland, Huntly Lodge, Fyvie Castle: all these were Georgiana's holy places, never out of mind. She wouldn't have liked Huntly Lodge's new look as a convention hotel, filled with business men, the air thick with cigarette smoke, paying its dues to the past with an abundance of Gordon tartan around the bar, and some antlered heads of deer, hanging slightly crooked in the entrance hall. One of the treasures of the National Portrait Gallery in Edinburgh is Romney's portrait of Georgiana's grandmother, the Duchess Jane, her young son standing beside her. As an illustration for my biography, this was one I really wanted. Having a colour transparency made, and paying the reproduction fee, didn't sound too bad in pounds sterling, but translated into our ailing dollars, it was a very expensive item.

Centuries of Gordon Castle estate books, recording the life of the ducal Gordon family, were held in Edinburgh. Much of it, in bound volumes, was in the neat handwriting of estate managers. Orderly columns of figures showed the annual gifts of firewood to the poor and life pensions for old nurses and gamekeepers. I unrolled thick parchment documents tied with pink ribbon, and heavily embossed pages of private letters. Without the help of a professional researcher, I would have been lost. Among the will and marriage settlements for innumerable Gordons we eventually found the documents which proved Georgiana McCrae's great expectations. Her father's intentions were clear, as was his affection, but he left it to his young wife to provide after his death for his three illegitimate children. And because she was childless, self-righteous and jealous of her husband's beautiful daughter, the Duchess found her solution in 'God's will' for Georgiana. Having expedited the McCraes' emigration, all the while encouraging them to believe in 'the good times coming', she appears to have decided that the promised legacy was not in Georgiana's best interests. Adding further injury, she gave the other two illegitimate children, Susan and Charles Gordon, a substantial inheritance.

As a contrast in settings, after wild Morayshire and Edinburgh's grey terraces, I had a tranquil, very English, week at the Crown and Anchor in Chichester, where the Goodwood Papers of the Dukes of Richmond and Gordon (heirs when the Gordon dukedom lapsed) held an unexpected cache of Gordon papers in the West Sussex record office. The evenings, so far south, were not as long as in Scotland, but there was plenty of light left to explore this impeccably maintained cathedral town, which even manages to hide its McDonald's behind a pale gold stone heritage facade, with a scarcely visible Big M sign. Each morning, as soon as the record office opened, I was in my place, with pencils sharpened for a full day's work. The Barsetshire novels gave instant recognition and I enjoyed my solitary week, with letters from long-dead Gordons to enliven the working hours.

After the serenity of West Sussex, I came home to confront the problem of Hugh McCrae's text. Before leaving I had broken the news of its unreliability to Janet Hay and her sister Anne Humphreys, copyright holders of Georgiana's words as well as those of their grandfather Hugh. That Hugh's and Georgiana's words were so entangled in the published *Journals* was a shock. They looked dismayed; and after the first uncertain words: 'Oh, naughty Hugh!' from Anne, we talked briefly about its implications for me. I couldn't quote from the printed text, and I would need to say something in a preface to explain why my quoted extracts might differ from the familiar words. I hadn't at that stage done a close comparison of the two versions and did not foresee the extent of the differences. The summer in London and Scotland, discovering the young artist and the Duke's daughter, deferred the problem, which faced me in mid-2003, when I began to write about Georgiana's colonial adventures. By that time I had a reliable text, typed from the manuscripts. Hugh McCrae, however, couldn't easily be dismissed. His 1934 text, reprinted in 1966, 1978, 1983 and 1992, had taken on a creative life of its own.

Without Hugh McCrae's edition of his grandmother's journals, she might well have been forgotten, and the house she designed would have been demolished. The Homestead at Arthur's Seat owed its survival to her great-grandson George McCrae who was prompted by the *Journals* to buy and restore the old family house during the 1960s. After George's death, his son Andrew gave the property to the National Trust, whose interest in maintaining it was almost certainly due to the history that went with it. Without that published history, no one would have thought to give Dromana West the official name McCrae. Over the years a series of guides at the Homestead had used Hugh McCrae's text as their bible, quoted from it as they showed visitors around. In turn the visitors bought the book at the Homestead. Libraries stocked it; school groups studied it as an accessible form of local history.

Having decided to forget Hugh McCrae's text and deal directly with Georgiana's own words on the page, I found that it wasn't so simple. Re-phrasing would not matter, nor would there be any embarrassment in replacing material I knew to have been omitted. The Duke of Gordon could at last be mentioned. But what to do about stories which seemed certain to be pure invention? Among the first to signal their absence were the much quoted entries for 12 and 16 November 1850. Valued by historians as first-hand accounts of Victoria's emergence as a colony, these have also suggested an interesting degree of intimacy between Georgiana and Governor La Trobe. I scanned the pages again, checked the dates, puzzled over the absences. For a time I speculated that the missing sentences could have been present in Georgiana's original, and censored when she made the fair copy that survived in manuscript. But, if so, where was the version from which Hugh McCrae took a delightfully lively early morning scene in which Georgiana stands beside La Trobe on the veranda at Jolimont. He wears a flowered dressing gown; together they listen to a serenading crowd until she leads him back into the house. Meanwhile Madame La Trobe, inside the house, has one of her neuralgic headaches.

Georgiana's account is much shorter. There is no flowered dressing gown. La Trobe does not hold her sleeve, nor does she lead him into the house. The reason for Georgiana's taking Madame La Trobe's place in the carriage for the opening of Princes Bridge is made plain, and she appears as a family friend, not a possible rival. Suspending judgement I began to compare other passages and found more discrepancies. I thought about the possible survival of the earlier text, censored but not burnt by Georgiana, and unknown to any family member except Hugh. It seemed unlikely. In the manuscript that has the guarantee of Georgiana's handwriting, there are passages which don't appear in Hugh McCrae's edited text. No great problem there, perhaps: he was trimming, and the nature of his choices showed how he wanted his grandmother to appear. But the additions, new stories, altered emphasis, witty phrases? Could they have been taken from the original journals, from which Georgiana made her fair copy? Both the nature and the extent of the differences ruled this out. The simple explanation was the right one. He was trying to liven up his book for publication and he had no sense of the integrity of a text.

My biography couldn't accommodate a close analysis of Hugh McCrae's text. It would disrupt the narrative and end in confusion if I were to alert the reader to every absence they might or might not have noticed, every addition that I had found to be an invention. In Georgiana's manuscript a certain Mr Montgomery is thrown from his horse. No story there. Hugh McCrae makes it a story by adding, 'Mr McCrae laughed'. Elsewhere Georgiana briefly refers to a neighbour's runaway mare. Again, no story. It is livened up by Hugh McCrae: 'all hands, except Mr McCrae, set out to catch the mare'. The cumulative effect of such small touches—and there are many of them—is to make Andrew McCrae more disagreeable than in his wife's text. The deletions were as eloquent as the insertions. A love poem written by Andrew to Georgiana for their fourteenth wedding anniversary was removed. So was an episode in which he showed pride in her paintings. Such changes did not make a vast difference to the impression, in Georgiana's text, of a difficult marriage, but Hugh McCrae's version simplified it by stressing Georgiana's forbearance and Andrew's bad temper.

The best way to deal with this tangle of competing texts was to use my endnotes for comment on certain passages, and only occasionally to confront Hugh McCrae in the narrative itself. The intimate moment with La Trobe was one which had to be dealt with in my text. I broke the news, disposed of the flowered dressing gown; and pointed out the unromantic truth that on Separation Day Georgiana was forty-six years old and six months pregnant with the last of her eight children. I used an endnote to contrast the compassion, noted in my text, which Georgiana showed in her shipboard entry for 30 October 1840, for 'poor people ... left dinnerless' with Hugh McCrae's 'drab and ugly crowd' who 'swarmed' on to the ship. I also endnoted the fact that Georgiana's reference to 'a young Israelite bound for Dublin on a mercantile trip' was turned by Hugh McCrae into 'a stout Hebrew merchant'. References to Aboriginal people were given a patronising edge that Georgiana never showed.

As a general warning, I did the best I could with a full-page Author's Note, prominently placed at the front of the biography, in the same typeface as the main narrative. This alerted readers to significant shifts in tone and emphasis, especially in Hugh McCrae's almost wholly negative construction of his grandfather. The McCrae copyright holders were not happy about the discovery of their grandfather's ventriloquism, but there was never any question of their persuading me to ignore it. Most remarkably, Janet Hay, on behalf of the estate, did not ask to read my book in advance of publication. She and other family members responded generously to my version of Georgiana; and if they were rueful or embarrassed about their grandfather's high-handed way with her journals, they didn't allow it to spoil the pleasure of having Georgiana's romantic early history verified in every detail.

There were still a few surprises after the publication of *Georgiana*. First, John Iremonger's misgivings were proved wrong. The first edition sold out before publication. Melbourne University Press (by then directed by Brian Wilder) had to ask the National Trust to lend one hundred copies so as to have a supply for the launch. Three hardcover reprints followed before the paperback, which also sold exceptionally well. The other surprise, to me at any rate, was that the Hugh McCrae story was not noticed by reviewers or anyone else. I'd blown the whistle, but it seemed that no one heard until 1998, when the *Oxford Companion to Australian History* referred to my having revealed 'a minor scandal'.

Six years after the publication of *Georgiana* the whole matter of the Hugh McCrae text was expertly examined in an outstanding PhD thesis by Thérèse Weber of the University of New South Wales. It made a fascinating story, and it is to be hoped that publication will follow, so that Georgiana's own words can be read. My one reservation about the thesis was its assumption that Hugh McCrae's daughter Huntly Cowper conspired with Beatrice Davis of Angus and Robertson to protect and reprint a text they knew to be flawed. There is no certainty that they examined the two texts, beyond making a few comparisons within the first section. The years from 1843 onwards were unavailable to them, having been sold to the collector Harry Chaplin. It seems unfair to blame Huntly Cowper and Beatrice Davis when dozens of historians—some of them very distinguished indeed—failed to look at the originals when they became available in the Fisher and the La Trobe libraries, and never questioned Hugh McCrae's editorial skills. As recently as 2002 Tim Flannery joined the company in *The Birth of Melbourne*, his anthology of writings about the city from its beginnings to the early twentieth century. Here it is again, that much anthologised McCrae piece, with the news of Separation brought to Jolimont by the mayor with his finger tied in a rag, holding an Adelaide newspaper. The injured finger, the ex-mayor's coughing,

La Trobe's neckerchief, and much more besides, is Hugh McCrae's exuberant invention.

My debt to Hugh McCrae is quite complicated. His misdemeanours as an editor created a colonial heroine for whose sake the McCrae Homestead was saved for posterity. Without the *Journals* and the Homestead, which gave Georgiana a place in colonial history, I would have had no subject—certainly no subject to interest a publisher. The effect on my way of seeing Georgiana is harder to assess. In some ways I was lucky, because in restoring what Hugh McCrae had discarded, I had the satisfaction of discovery. Because he was creating a book specifically for the 1934 centenary of Victoria's settlement, he suppressed or played down the homesickness of Georgiana, in whom I found an unremitting sense of exile. Because he couldn't reveal her parentage, he left out her hopes of a legacy from her father's wife, and the disappointment—even the rage—with which she took in the bad news of the Duchess's will. Why he chose to make Andrew McCrae so grumpy is hard to say, except to underline the strength of the stoic Georgiana, or perhaps to validate some family stories.

My version of Andrew McCrae restores some softer moments and, because I was free to write about the ducal background, the complexities of Georgiana's story emerged more clearly. Most important, probably, was the shift in emphasis from pioneer to painter. My encounter with Hugh McCrae's Georgiana has many parallels in life writing, such as the example of modern biographers of Jane Austen who have revised and reinterpreted the insipid version left by Austen family members. Yet there is one difference. The first person voice and the diary form give a semblance of authority against which the biography struggles to compete. It's easy enough to change the lighting, but the advantage remains with a ventriloquist.

8

Group Portrait: The Boyds

'So you're writing a Boyd biography. Which Boyd?' 'Well, I thought ... all of them.' '*All* of them?' The tone is one of surprise rather than disapproval but it does suggest that 'all the Boyds' might be a folly. 'Terrific subject, but how will you get them all in?' was another comment. Of course these doubts echoed my own. Five generations and a time span of nearly two centuries, ceaseless travelling between Europe and Australia, and dozens of individual life stories, all worth the telling: wasn't this, well, a bit much?

The story of the Boyd family of artists would tempt any biographer. There's an obvious fascination in a family for whose members, over five generations, a life in art has presented itself as the obvious way to live. Some have chosen other paths, and for them the collective signifier 'the Boyds' is probably unwelcome. But ever since 1886 when painter Minnie à Beckett married painter Arthur Merric Boyd there has been an extraordinary flowering of talent. In painting, pottery, sculpture, architecture and writing, the creativity of the Boyds has been a phenomenon in Australian cultural life. Merric the potter, Penleigh the landscape painter and Martin the novelist made their mark in the early twentieth century. In the next generation Merric's son, painter Arthur Boyd, was a national figure; so was Penleigh's son, architect and writer Robin Boyd. Arthur's younger brothers, Guy the sculptor and David the painter and potter, complete a remarkable quartet. Marriages brought more artists into the family circle: Merric's wife Doris Gough and Penleigh's wife Edith Anderson were painters. Arthur married painter Yvonne Lennie. David's wife Hermia Lloyd Jones was a ceramic artist and sculptor. Lucy Boyd, herself a talented artist, married potter Hatton Beck. Mary Boyd's first husband was painter John Perceval; and she later married painter Sidney Nolan.

It's almost enough just to list the members of the Boyd family to show their attraction for a biographer and the difficulty of the subject. Some biographies die on the page for lack of narrative interest: this one might have too much. The traditional biography takes one central figure and moves inexorably from cradle to grave. Parents and grandparents, brothers and sisters, husbands and wives may be included as supporting cast. Sometimes a marriage gives a double focus. Nigel Nicolson's biography of his parents, Harold Nicolson and Vita Sackville-West, is one example. Family biographies? The Brontë sisters have been 'done' individually and as a trio. Three sisters who were seldom parted from one another, stayed for the most part in the family house, and all died young: their story can be told well or badly but it doesn't present serious structural problems. Nearer in time to the Boyds are the Lamberts, whose three-generation story has been told by Andrew Motion. But *The Lamberts* follows a straight vertical line from painter George to his musician son Constant and grandson Kit, manager of the rock group Who. It doesn't stretch horizontally as the Boyd story would need to do. Penelope Fitzgerald's *The Knox Brothers* works brilliantly, but it concentrates on one generation and it is an insider's perspective. Born a Knox, Fitzgerald was writing about her father and his brothers. Her book was shaped by memory and a heritage of family stories, and given unity by its narrator's viewpoint. Barbara Caine's *Bombay to Bloomsbury: the Stracheys* (2005), with its long line of siblings, shows their distinctive qualities in impressive depth as well as breadth but her thematic approach doesn't avoid some repetition.

I first thought about a Boyd group biography when I was writing the life of Martin Boyd. I met his sister, his nephews and nieces and some of his cousins; and I read a great deal of family history, which was one of Martin Boyd's passions. It was important to know that history, not least because in various guises it informed his novels.

To know what stories he told and what he bypassed or suppressed was a way towards understanding Martin himself. When I talked to Arthur Boyd about his uncle he confirmed that the opening pages of *The Cardboard Crown* were more or less factual: that the discovery of Martin's grandmother's diaries had taken place in the à Beckett family house in 1948, and that Arthur himself had urged Martin to make a novel out of them. Arthur's annotations, in the margins of the photocopied pages I sent him, include a disclaimer of one remark: ('I always thought the Left was right') which 'would have been a bit cheeky'. Because Arthur had never been told the secret of Emma à Beckett's parentage, he couldn't understand why Martin seemed reluctant to write her story.

Writing Martin Boyd's life in the mid-1980s, I felt the hidden story straining to be told. I would have liked to explore the influence of Emma Mills, her very new money and its 'convict taint' on her descendants. The strength and intelligence of the convict's daughter could be seen in her diaries; so could her generosity, and her active interest in the arts. Unusual for a woman of her time, she was the family banker and business woman from the age of twenty-one. The value of her father's legacy in city property, including the Melbourne Brewery, grew with 'Marvellous Melbourne'; and even after the crash of the 1890s diminished her income she was still able to support her family in considerable luxury. Her husband never worked, nor did her sons, while the allowances paid to her four daughters left the sons-in-law free from any need for paid employment. She encouraged her daughter Minnie to develop her talents as an artist; and when Minnie married artist Arthur Merric Boyd, Emma's ample purse provided for their needs. One of her last acts, not long before her death, was to pay her schoolboy grandson Penleigh Boyd five shillings for a little sketch.

From time to time I thought about writing Emma's story, but I didn't want to revisit *The Cardboard Crown* with an implied rebuke to Martin for having dodged the convict issue. I was more interested in following the intertwined threads of art and money and the effect of a family secret. Did the children of Emma à Beckett know that their privileges and pleasures stemmed directly from a convict's accumulation in land and the liquor trade? It is hard to believe that her sons and daughters knew nothing; but except for Martin, who kept his discoveries to himself, the later generations almost certainly remained in ignorance of this shaping force in their history.

Without the convict legacy, and without Emma's vigorous promotion of her daughter's career, would we have had the exquisite landscapes of Minnie Boyd, or Arthur Merric Boyd's serene studies of light on water? The remnants of Emma's fortune gave their three sons, Merric, Penleigh and Martin, a degree of independence. Not so for the next generation. Merric's children, Lucy, Arthur, Guy, David and Mary grew up in poverty: they had to make their way through talent and energy. Penleigh's son Robin was the first Boyd of his generation to take paid employment; before being articled as an architect he was an office boy at fifteen shillings a week. Arthur, aged fourteen, worked in a factory; Guy and David took labouring jobs; Lucy worked as a nanny. For all of them the commitment to art remained. The brilliant careers of the postwar period made 'the Boyds' a phenomenon, in which the individual and collective stories offered material for half a dozen biographies.

It took me a long time to see how the material could be shaped. Not that I thought of it so often: I was busy with other projects. My biography of Georgiana McCrae made me think about the conditions in which an artist might flourish or—like Georgiana—be constrained. Compared with the Boyd story, *Georgiana* was an easy book to shape. A single focus, with Georgiana always at the centre, gave a clear narrative line: the contingent life around her gave patches of colour but did not distract. In effect I wrote the story backwards, starting with an image of an old woman in suburban Melbourne in 1887, having her portrait painted. That episode, with Georgiana's reflections at the age of eighty-three, occupied the first few pages; and the rest of the book, having taken her back to childhood, career as a painter, marriage, motherhood and emigration, came full circle to the old woman of the opening scene. Could I use that form for Emma à Beckett? Perhaps, but because I saw Emma's achievement as the founding of a family of artists it could not end with her death. Besides, after two single-focus biographies I wanted to try a group portrait.

One possibility was a mother–daughter study: a double focus with Emma à Beckett and Minnie Boyd as the central figures, perhaps suggesting their legacy to sons and grandsons. That, I thought, would work only if the careers of the later Boyds, especially the major achievements of Arthur and Robin Boyd, had been fully documented. From Franz Philipp to Grazia Gunn, art critics had given fine studies of Arthur Boyd's work in which the context of time and place and the private self were perceptively considered. Yet in the absence of a full Arthur Boyd biography, a companion study for Geoffrey Serle's *Robin Boyd* (1995) and my own *Martin Boyd* (1988), it seemed premature to write the lives of the Boyd matriarchs.

With a family biography, the traditional birth-to-death time line won't work: a family has no discernible beginning and no end. A series of glimpses, as if with a hand-held camera? No, not a Boyd home movie; the stories were too complex. An unfolding: that was what I wanted, but where to start? One scene presented itself as a way in to the story: the wedding day of Emma Mills, the convict's daughter. There are obvious dramatic possibilities in the moment when Emma, beautiful and intelligent, with a young lady's education, great wealth and an unmentionable past, crossed the invisible line of class to enter the formidable à Beckett family. That's where a film might start, but as I began to think of it in visual terms it seemed in danger of being predictable: something like *The Valley of Decision*, a 1940s family saga with Greer Garson ageing gracefully over three generations. In the twenty-first century that wouldn't do.

If I could find a way to tell it, there was a wonderful New World story in the collision between the world of Sir William à Beckett and that of Emma's father, the convict from a labouring family who made a New World fortune after serving his sentence. And as I thought about the other marriage that created the à Beckett–Boyd family, it also took on representative meaning. Lucy Martin, who eloped with Captain John Theodore Boyd in 1857, was the daughter of Dr Robert Martin, medical practitioner turned squatter, who came overland with cattle from Sydney in 1839 and took up large landholdings in Port Phillip. The Irish-born army officer Boyd was second in command of the military escort on a ship which brought convicts to Van Diemen's Land in 1845. Judge and squatter, soldier and convict: these were the forebears of the Boyds. This, surely, was where a biography of the Boyds should begin. Like the nursery counting game of 'tinker, tailor …', or a set of playing cards, this quartet of pioneers made a matched set, as symmetrical as any novelist's contrivance. Was there a chance that they would emerge from the public records of their day with some degree of individuality? At the risk of writing the dull section which readers skim, wanting the real story to begin, I decided that a family biography had to start with these four men in their New World roles.

So I had a beginning: three ships sailing into Port Phillip Bay and a party of overlanders from Sydney.

Two marriages in the 1850s: Emma Mills and W.A.C. à Beckett, Lucy Martin and John Theodore Boyd. And, in 1886, the marriage of Minnie à Beckett and Arthur Merric Boyd, both artists. Their sons, Merric, Penleigh and Martin, their daughter Helen. Their grandchildren: Penleigh's sons, Merric's sons and daughters, Helen's children. In surveying that troop of Boyd descendants I began to worry that there were too many stories. Henry James' words for an over-crowded narrative came to mind: 'a loose and baggy monster' or (even worse) 'a fluid pudding'. Or—someone's jibe at the shapeless family novel—a Forsyte sago.

In writing Martin Boyd's story I had found a major theme in the importance of the family house. Returning to Australia in 1948, having made his name in England as a novelist, Martin bought his à Beckett grandfather's house, The Grange, Harkaway, in the hope of making it the family centre it had been in his childhood. This gesture—a folly as it turned out—echoed an earlier attempt to repossess the past. In 1890 Martin's grandfather W.A.C. à Beckett bought back Penleigh House in Wiltshire, the à Beckett estate which he always believed was his by right. Because W.A.C.'s grandfather had not married the mother of his children, the Australian branch of the family was outside the legitimate line, and the Penleigh estate went to a cousin. Emma à Beckett's inheritance bought Penleigh House for her family, but when the economic crash of the 1890s reduced her income a choice had to be made between England and Australia. The family could not keep up two houses. Melbourne-born Emma never liked the Wiltshire manor house. It was her decision to sell it; her husband, who had been spending recklessly in England, had to agree. The à Becketts, with the Boyds and their children, returned to Australia.

Looking through a Boyd family album I saw visual evidence of the difference between life at Penleigh House and at the bayside suburb of Sandringham where the Boyds lived on their return. A photograph of Merric Boyd in a sailor suit and wide-brimmed hat, with his brother Penleigh in a magnificent pram, both attended by a neat and watchful nanny, contrasts with a later image of the boys climbing on the rocks at Sandringham. The hand that held the camera was at some distance from the adventurous children; the effect is that of untrammelled freedom. If they had grown up at Penleigh House, sitting each Sunday in the squire's pew, boarding at an English public school, the two boys might still have been artists but their shaping influences would have been quite different—and Australian cultural history would have been much diminished.

In Martin Boyd's novels Penleigh House appears in idealised guise as Waterpark, and he never ceased to hope that one of his nephews would bring it back into the family. The tenacity with which the Boyds held on to the idea of the family house was evident too in Guy Boyd's impulsive return from Toronto, where his career in sculpture was flourishing, in order to buy back his Boyd grandfather's house in Sandringham in 1981.

This undistinguished Federation-style villa held such happy memories of Guy's childhood that he moved his family across the world in order to save it from developers, restore it and live in it. And when David Boyd returned to Sydney after great success in Europe, he and his wife Hermia chose a house large enough to become a gallery, where young painters could show their work, and where their collection of Boyd family paintings could be secured against dispersion.

An earlier example was The Robins, Warrandyte, the house built by Penleigh Boyd for his wife and children, idealised and yearned for when Penleigh went to war in 1915, but sold when marriage and career faltered after his return. In an effort to recapture marital happiness Penleigh bought back the house in 1923. His romantic gesture failed: he died in a car crash later the same year, his marriage still in disarray.

In 1993 Arthur Boyd made a splendid act of dispossession in giving his Bundanon homestead and property on the Shoalhaven River in New South Wales to the Australian people. This took on added meaning in the context of earlier family houses. Arthur never stopped grieving for the loss of Open Country, his father's house and pottery at Murrumbeena. Sold in 1963 and demolished by developers, it remained in memory as a lost paradise of childhood. By giving away Bundanon and the collection of family paintings it housed, Arthur made them safe from destruction. But, unlike Martin and Penleigh, he did not try to hold on to the past. 'To give something you've got to lose it', he said. 'That's what I reckon it's all about.'

The Bundanon gift, I thought, would be the way to end a Boyd family biography: an open ending with ongoing life and art implied, and links with previous generations affirmed through the thousands of Boyd works of art, letters, photographs and catalogues housed in the Bundanon archive. By good fortune the diaries of Emma à Beckett are there too, back from nearly half a century of journeyings in Europe since Martin took them from The Grange in 1951. Having first read them on microfiche in the National Library, I had the full sense of the physical reality of the little closely written volumes when I re-read them at Bundanon, within sight of the Shoalhaven River, while staying in the old house which Arthur Boyd had reclaimed.

A beginning and an ending: but what about the intervening chapters? Fifteen major characters at least, and five generations. Henry James' warnings about 'loose and baggy monsters' stirred a memory of a series of conversations in 1976 with James' biographer, Leon Edel.

Edel talked about his work in progress: a book about the Bloomsbury group. With a vast archive and at least nine major characters, he had structural problems which he had just then triumphantly resolved. He would choose certain episodes in the lives of his nine Bloomsberries, and 'string them together as one strings beads'. 'When the string is complete and harmonious each bead has a relation to the other beads on the string'.[1] I remember

Edel's delight in the image of the string of beads. As we crossed the Melbourne suburbs together in the half hour's drive between his city hotel and Monash, Edel told me the title he had chosen. It was *Bloomsbury: a House of Lions*. When it was published in 1979 I was reminded of its author's creative excitement and his insistence on the imaginative use of form in biography. Twenty-five years later, the string of beads idea, together with the house of Edel's title, gave the hint I needed to write the Boyd biography.

My string of beads would be a sequence of houses. The idea of the house as an image of self is a familiar one, but it seemed especially appropriate for the Boyds. For each of them the choice of a house represented something different. The dream of repossessing the past is not uncommon; what makes the Boyds remarkable is the tenacity with which so many of them pursued it. The choice of one or two significant houses for each of the Boyd artists would shape the biography; it would also define character and express a way of life. Instead of reducing the Boyds to the dreaded fluid pudding, I hoped to show their distinctive personalities and achievements. What better than the family house to show how they lived and what they lived for?

After the initial excitement at the idea of the family house, I had to look at realities. Who, after all, were 'The Boyds'? Not the whole extended family, not every descendant of Arthur Merric and Emma Minnie Boyd, but the professional artists who made their names individually as well as collectively in pottery, painting, writing and architecture, and whose careers were completed, or nearly so. The first trio of brothers chose themselves: Merric, Penleigh and Martin. Less obvious was the late-flowering talent of their sister Helen Read, who painted under her married name, avoided being publicised as a Boyd, and was never widely known. In the next generation, Merric's three sons, Arthur, Guy and David, were all fully committed to a public career. With their cousin Robin the architect they made up the collective entity known as 'The Boyds'.

Almost inevitably, given the time and place, the high-achieving Boyds were all men. Could I redress the balance? What about Merric's daughter Lucy, who had a long creative life as a potter in partnership with her husband Hatton Beck? And her sister Mary, wife of John Perceval, and later of Sidney Nolan? And Robin Boyd's older brother Pat, who studied at the Melbourne Gallery School in the mid-1930s? Perhaps we lost another Boyd painter when Pat Boyd enrolled in the RAAF in 1939. Having served with great distinction, he maintained his passion for flying and when the war ended he became a test pilot for a commercial airline. He died in 1980, never having developed his early promise as an artist.

Pondering these fine distinctions, I decided that for my purposes 'The Boyds' meant the nine professional artists, Arthur Merric and Emma Minnie, Merric, Penleigh, Martin, Robin, Arthur, Guy and David. Eight men, only one woman. Yet in telling the family stories I could show

how and why it was that none of the younger Boyd women had the independent status that Emma Minnie Boyd, with her mother's wealth and patronage, achieved as early as the 1880s. I could point to the evidence of talent, and take as a telling example the only work by Mary Boyd to be held in any public collection. Her expressionist painting, *Hands*, in the Heide Museum of Modern Art, is powerful and remarkably assured. It was painted when Mary Boyd was only fifteen. Who can say whether she could or would have matched her brothers in creativity?

I was tempted to write Mary Boyd's story as that of the artist's wife. I had visited her in the mid-1980s at the Nolan manor house, The Rodd, on the Welsh borders, to talk about her uncle Martin. Even in that short interview, Sidney Nolan took over. Charming and eloquent, he drew the conversation to himself while his wife went out to make coffee, and held it when she returned. Her brief comments on her uncle Martin were perceptive; it was tantalising to have so little from her and so much from Nolan, who somehow switched the conversation to Dostoevsky. The Rodd overflowed with Nolan's work; it could not be called a Boyd house, except tangentially. But the path Mary Boyd took from her father's shabby Murrumbeena pottery to Sidney Nolan's emblem of success, The Rodd, fitted my idea of suggesting a way of life through the choice of a house.

Uncertain about the Boyd sisters, I wrote to them both. A telephone call from Lucy Beck left no doubt about her feelings. She had always avoided the public attention to 'The Boyds', she said, and it would distress her to be put in the limelight. She would help in any way she could with her parents and her brothers' stories, but 'please, leave me out'. Mary Nolan did not reply. Their aunt Helen Read was more forthcoming. She talked freely and happily about herself, her mother Emma Minnie, and her own unwillingness as a young woman to be conscripted into the family business of painting. One thing she was sure about: she was a Boyd, and proud of it, but she was not one of 'The Boyds'. Nor was her daughter, the talented graphic artist Gayner Read, whose work in stained glass I saw in Helen Read's house. The other Boyd women, those who married into the family, made a remarkable group, all highly intelligent, all committed to their husbands' careers. My chosen structure, in the family house, gave me a chance to show how much, and in what distinctive ways, Yvonne, Phyllis, Hermia and Patricia Boyd shaped 'The Boyds'.

By moving through the decades while shifting the scene from one house to another I hoped to give a sense of evolving character. There would be no cradle-to-grave self-contained narratives. Instead, there would be a series of glimpses of each of the Boyds at different stages of life, and seen in their developing relationships to the others. To take one example: Penleigh Boyd appears first as an adventurous small boy in his grandparents' houses in Wiltshire and Brighton. Aged fifteen he is seen with his brothers at Yarra Glen, longing to leave school to be a painter. As grandson, son and brother, Penleigh's personality is established in a series of vignettes before he moves from the edges of other family narratives to take centre stage in his own chapter. As one reviewer of *The Boyds* remarked: 'Everyone is everyone else's hinterland'.

As I counted the names for my list of characters I pondered the corresponding houses. Architectural merit was irrelevant. Which ones best suggested the individuality of each Boyd and the way of life each one chose? Which houses were still there to be visited? And for those that had not survived, what documentation in manuscripts, photographs or living memory could be found? Miraculously, I had a high level of success with houses in and near Melbourne. Glenfern, the neo-Gothic mansion in East St Kilda where Arthur Merric Boyd grew up in the 1870s, now belongs to the National Trust, and is used as a centre for musicians and writers. Wilton, the à Beckett house in Brighton, survives with a change of name and some alterations; so does Tralee, the Boyd farm at Yarra Glen. Penleigh Boyd's Warrandyte house and the garden he created are scarcely altered. The two that are lost happen to be the ones to which the strongest memories attach themselves.

Behind Bundanon, the Shoalhaven property which we can all visit, is the unvisitable Open Country where the Boyd children played and painted and shaped clay for the potter's wheel in the 1920s and 1930s. The other lost house which carried its full freight of memory was The Grange at Harkaway, built by W.A.C. and Emma à Beckett in 1866. This unpretentious country dwelling was the family centre for the children and grandchildren of two generations, and the scene of Martin Boyd's ill-fated attempt, in 1948–52, to reclaim the past. Although I had already written about Martin at the Grange, my research for *The Boyds* altered my perceptions quite radically. I had thought of the restoration of the old house as a sad failure for Martin Boyd, who could not bring back the family life he remembered. And so it was. But I hadn't taken into account the resentment of some of his cousins who saw Martin's elegantly refurbished Grange as a travesty of the house they loved. When I talked to his cousin Joan à Beckett Minson, then in her nineties, I understood far better the passionate attachments which had grown up over nearly a century of family history. Every corner had its memories—and Martin had swept them all away with his fastidious neo-Georgian broom.

Travelling in England, with four houses to explore, I was greeted by the polite but puzzled owner of Penleigh House in Wiltshire, the ancestral manor house, dating from Elizabethan times, which was briefly reclaimed in the 1890s by W.A.C. à Beckett. Touring it from cellars to attics, I could see the way of life described in Emma à Beckett's diaries. A dozen Boyd paintings took on new dimensions, as did the 'Waterpark' scenes in Martin Boyd's Langton novels. When the present owner, a London lawyer, understood what this seemingly eccentric Australian writer wanted, she became fully engaged in the quest for the 1890s house and the village life that went with it. Later that month I made a return visit to Cambridgeshire where Martin Boyd's friends, who still remember him with affection, offered a guided tour of his Little Eversden cottage.

In London, too, I was lucky in finding that David Boyd's early Victorian terrace in Islington was still owned by the people who had bought it from him in 1971. They knew its history; they described the neighbours who were there in the Boyds' time, and they were especially acute in their perceptions of the characteristic tone of 1960s Islington, long before Tony Blair moved in. The Boyds had liked Islington because it wasn't posh. Today it is very posh, very polished. The present owners documented its 1960s scruffiness and the multiracial mix that included a black American bare-fist boxer, several West Indies families and many Greek Cypriots. They showed me the walled garden Hermia Boyd designed and the broken place in a marble mantlepiece which David had repaired and painted in marble texture over white stucco. They remembered the creative clutter of paintings and the kiln that barely fitted in the coal cellar. The plum tree Hermia planted still flourished, but her romantically conceived camomile lawn and greengage tree were gone.

In search of Arthur Boyd's London years I visited his painter son Jamie, who exemplified my sense of the family's tenacious hold on their chosen dwellings. Jamie still lives with his wife and children in Hampstead Lane, Highgate, in the house that Arthur and Yvonne Boyd bought soon after arrival in London in 1959. Touring the rooms with Jamie was an education in a painter's use of space. Arthur Boyd's work had overflowed from room to room, from basement to attics. One room was kept 'more or less pristine' for prospective buyers and dealers. All the rest, in varying degrees, were invaded. With a kiln outside the kitchen door, a lithographic press in the ground-floor sitting room, with sheets of copper, rolls of canvas, stacks of boards in every room, the Boyds' living space was pervaded by the artist's energy and its physical expression. Life and work were indivisible, as the Hampstead house plainly showed.

Back in Australia, I had still to see the houses Robin Boyd designed and built for himself and his family. As with his artist cousins, the life and work were indivisible. Robin Boyd's 1947 Camberwell house belongs to the early years of his marriage and career. Like its successor in South Yarra, completed almost a decade later, it embodies the architect's ideas at the time of building. When Robin Boyd's widow Patricia showed me the South Yarra house, where she still lived, thirty years after his death, she gave a sense of the excitement it created in the 1950s, as an experiment in living and an adventure in modernist design. The personal element was expressed by Robin Boyd himself when he described the unifying timber-lined catenary roof which joined two pavilions—one of them the children's domain—in one house. The tension, Boyd said, was symbolic:

> Here was a family plan based on convictions of anti-togetherness: parents' and children's blocks were planned to be separated by a court for mutual privacy. Yet it was still intended to be one shared home … Today, the cables [of the roof] almost literally hold the family together.[2]

Like his uncle Martin, though with more intellectual precision, Robin Boyd understood and wrote about the 'strange kind of possessive love mankind has always had for his dwelling'.[3] His attachment to his own dwellings, however, differed from that of most of the other Boyds in that each house was his creation. From his great-grandfather to his uncle Martin and his cousin Guy, other family members were reclaiming, conserving, holding on. Arthur Boyd saw things differently: he found a creative way to join past and future, by giving away his Shoalhaven house. Robin Boyd, too, created for the future. If he had lived longer, he would have moved on from the tension roof of his South Yarra house. His legacy includes many ideas for living, in houses designed for others. His classic work *Australia's Home* (1952) is unsurpassed for its insight into Australian domestic architecture. When I met Robin Boyd's son Penleigh, also an architect, he quoted Churchill's remark: 'We shape our houses and afterwards they shape us'. That line stayed with me as a succinct way of expressing my idea for the group study of the family. Like Edel's Bloomsbury biography it would offer psychological interpretation within an episodic structure.

Robin Boyd's two houses were the latest and last in my set of Boyd dwellings: my string of beads. For the Australian family's founding fathers I found ample documentation in public records. John Mills appeared in Gloucestershire police reports and convict musters; Sir William à Beckett in portraits, memoirs, legal judgments and newspaper columns. The first Boyd to land in Australia (Major Alexander Boyd, father of Captain Boyd of Glenfern) was represented by a portrait and a set of entries in the Devonshire regimental archives at Exeter which documented his service in the colony. Dr Robert Martin's land holdings and business activities filled letter books and ledgers in the papers of his agent James Graham, held by the University of Melbourne. But, as to dwellings, I couldn't hope for much. There was only Liardet's sketch of John Mills' Melbourne brewery and a photograph in the State Library which might have been Sir William à Beckett's East Melbourne house, but probably wasn't.

One evening in 1998, idly watching an ABC television news report, I was suddenly alerted by a familiar name: Dr Martin of Viewbank. An archaeological team directed by Heritage Victoria was excavating the site of Dr Martin's house in Heidelberg, Victoria. The site was chosen as one of the very few examples of Melbourne's early pastoral period which had not been looted or developed. The dig, as the TV footage demonstrated, had exposed a cellar, six feet deep, and other evidence of a large establishment. Fragments of elaborate cornices and marble mantelpieces were retrieved. Scraps of wallpaper, broken cups and plates from a dinner service of fine china with a pattern of flowers, made in England, came to the surface. A set of five bells and a tangle of bell pulls recalled the servants who waited on Dr Martin and his family. Children's toys evoked the family life of Viewbank. All this brought to unexpected light the house from which Lucy Martin eloped to marry Captain John Theodore Boyd in 1857. This romance, adapted by Martin Boyd for an early scene in *The Montforts*, was commemorated in the family by giving the first daughter in each generation the name of Lucy.

The archaeological dig at Viewbank, perfectly timed to coincide with my own archival research, was magical. I had wanted one of the earliest houses, and here it was, emerging from the soil, to be photographed and analysed by experts as an example of 1840s pastoral living. For me it had an added resonance. I saw myself again, a small child, enchanted and frustrated by the shapes and colours of broken china dug up on the site of our own house in Studley Park Road in 1935. I couldn't match the pieces then. Now, though well aware of the limits of reconstruction, I could look for a pattern in the fragments of Dr Martin's 1840s house at Heidelberg.

9

Face to Face: Judy Cassab

Just after *Martin Boyd* was published I said with absolute certainty in a radio interview, that I would never write the biography of a living person. I spoke confidently about the virtue of detachment, the need to stand back and see the completed life in context. Writing about the living, I thought, was likely to be controlled by the subject. At best it would be respectful and cautious; at worst it would be authorised gossip or ventriloquism. A celebrity life of a pop star or sporting hero would always have a market, but its value would be ephemeral, its reading of personality inevitably shallow, and often offensively intrusive. All this I now would qualify. Indeed I must, because I have written the life of the artist Judy Cassab, and based it on many interviews with her, as well as her private diaries and other sources in the here-and-now of her daily life.

Although I still believe that there are big risks inherent in the biography of a living person, I now know that detachment is not an absolute, and that the gulf of time between author and subject does not mean the withdrawal of the writing self into some enclave of objectivity. It is not possible to spend years on biographical research and writing without becoming very closely committed to an idea of personality, a way of seeing, that is one's own construction. Nor is it desirable. As Richard Holmes has said, 'Empathy is the most powerful, the most necessary, and the most deceptive, of all biographical emotions'.[1] Without the capacity to stand, at least from moment to moment, in the subject's shoes, and to see, however imperfectly, as that person might have seen, the biography cannot come to life. Somewhere between detachment and identification is the biographer's shaky ground.

The two extremes of a biographical relationship are the worshipful and the destructive. As in life, so in biography. Beware of idealisation, keep clear of the vendetta. But these and other elements in the relationship between writer and subject are everyday hazards in any human exchange. The biographer has no monopoly on possessiveness ('Virginia Woolf belongs to ME') or narcissism, in which the gaze gives back one's own reflection.

I had not measured the risks of writing the biography of Judy Cassab in mid-2002, when I made one of the most impulsive telephone calls of my life to ask this celebrated portrait painter if she would 'sit' for me. She was astonished; and when our brief conversation ended, so was I, as I began to think about what I had done. I did not know Judy well; I hadn't thought about the sources of her biography; and I had scarcely discussed the idea with anyone, least of all a publisher. Nothing in my background prepared me to write a life which begins in Vienna in 1920 and which crosses continents many times before the end of the twentieth century. I would have to explore a Jewish–Hungarian childhood, and enter imaginatively into the Second World War experiences of a woman whose family was murdered in Auschwitz. Migration to Australia in 1951 brought Cassab closer but there was still an abyss between my own sedate and sheltered Catholic childhood in middle-class Melbourne, where sameness was taken for granted, and Judy Cassab's world of loss and displacement.

If my telephone call to Cassab was impulsive, so was her approach to me, six years earlier. It was mid-1996 in Canberra, where we had both been invited to speak at a National Library seminar, 'Constructing a Life'. Judy's paper was on portrait painting, mine on biography. I talked about Georgiana McCrae's predicament, exiled in 1840s Melbourne, forbidden by her husband, even in a time of near-bankruptcy, to use her art of portraiture because 'a gentleman's wife did not paint for money'. Judy joined the discussion vigorously: 'If my husband did not let me paint, I would be divorced!'

We listened to one another's papers, spoke briefly during one of the breaks, and that might have been the end of our acquaintanceship if the National Library hadn't done our bookings and placed us in the same hotel. Next morning, both of us ready for departure, we had time to spare—Judy is as unfailingly, incurably, punctual as I am—and so we sat over breakfast and talked.

Judy hadn't then read my biography of Georgiana McCrae, and as she listened to my talk at the Library, her attention had been caught by my account of the dilemma she herself had faced: that of reconciling marriage and motherhood with a commitment to an artist's life. Judy's own diaries—a selection from fifty years of almost daily entries—had been published in the previous year, not long after *Georgiana*, and I had reviewed the book for the *Sunday Age* in Melbourne. If she remembered the review, she would have known that I was interested in her life and work. But that interest was nothing unusual. After half a century of media attention, the publishing success of the Cassab *Diaries* was simply one more endorsement of her place in Australian cultural life.

I can't remember what else we talked about that morning in Canberra. We had said goodbye in the lobby, but as I waited for my taxi to the airport Judy reappeared to ask me if I would sit to her for a non-commissioned portrait. She explained that each year she chose a few sitters, and that because no money changed hands she could enjoy painting the subject, experimenting as she pleased, without constraint. I was taken aback. I had never thought of a portrait of myself; and I have never much liked being photographed. And yet I was flattered by the invitation; and the thought of being painted by someone of Cassab's high reputation was hard to resist. I knew that Cassab had won the Archibald Prize for portraiture twice, and that in the long history of that award she was the only woman to have done so. The list of her subjects, as I later discovered, is a roll-call of the famous in public life and in the arts. This was an opportunity to see an artist at work from a privileged position. I was too astonished to agree at once: Judy gave me her card, and I telephoned her a few days afterwards to make plans. Later that year I went to Sydney for my sittings in the studio at Judy's apartment in Double Bay.

By chance, I knew Double Bay well, and it made a link with Judy Cassab to discover that some of my favourite places there were hers too. Years earlier, while I was in Sydney to interview some of the friends of Martin Boyd, I had been staying in a hotel in the central part of the city, which I found noisy, airless and oppressive. Someone suggested I move out to Double Bay for some peace and quiet, close to the sea. It worked. Although Double Bay is undeniably a place for the affluent, the shops and other buildings are mostly small scale: it feels like a village. From my base in a friendly little hotel in Knox Street, I found several coffee shops where people sit and read newspapers, European style. There was a first-class bookshop for browsing (Lesley McKay's, now no longer there) and for dining alone in the evening I felt very much at home at the '21' on Knox Street, famous for its *wiener schnitzel* with mashed potato, and its clientèle of elderly Hungarians.

After dinner, while the light lasted on the long summer evenings, I used to walk down Ocean Avenue to the waterfront, and sit on one of the benches, watching the little boats rock gently in the shallows. This became my Sydney routine: the best possible retreat into thought and silence after a day of interviews. Watching the boats on Double Bay was the way to relax after a day with strangers, trying to balance the necessary prepared questions with the need to be alert for the unexpected revelation, and to be a good listener rather than a more or less animated tape-recorder. For my first sitting in Judy Cassab's studio, I had only to stroll a block or two up the hill in Ocean Avenue, a walk I had taken many times without knowing that Cassab and her husband lived there. I discovered that they called '21' their second dining room; their crowded bookshelves were filled from Lesley McKay's bookshop, and their ritual morning or afternoon walk to the water's edge was the same as mine.

For a biographer, fresh from interviewing members of the Boyd family, the reversal of roles was easily done. I didn't have to prepare anything, and the only preliminary was a phone call from Judy Cassab to ask what I planned to wear. I had brought a silk blouse, patterned in rich, deep colours which I thought might appeal to her, but she firmly dismissed this idea as 'too strong a note'. We settled on blue, soft and clear, not too emphatic.

The sittings were perfectly programmed, although they seemed spontaneous. I was a few minutes early but

Judy Cassab was waiting for me. Her blue and white Meissen coffee cups were laid out on a tray, ready for the mid-session break, with strong coffee in a thermos, and a plate of small sugared biscuits. I thought we would talk only at half time, but not so; we talked as she painted, throughout the sitting. Seated comfortably, I didn't feel posed. Judy made it clear that a turn of the head, a movement of the hands would not disturb her in the least. She was not only painting my portrait; she was getting to know me. It was not very different from my own approach to interviewing. I make my notes while letting the tape recorder run unchecked. Judy makes her brushstrokes as she listens and asks questions. She sees this interchange as essential to her task:

> I am passionately interested in people's childhood, why they chose the path they are on, how they met their spouses, and hundreds of other things [and] for me it's as if each word lands on the tip of my brush and is then transferred to the canvas.[2]

Cassab compares the relationship between painter and sitter with that of the therapist and the patient. Where else, she asks, can you speak as freely as in the studio, when the painter gives full attention to the inner life that she hopes to create with her brush? Total concentration on you, on your feelings, your individuality: that is what she offers. For these brief hours you are the most important person in the world: how can you resist the invitation to talk freely? Indeed, few people can resist;

and that's why Judy Cassab's sitters become her friends. This would not be true of all portrait painters, nor do all of them allow such freedom of speech and movement to the sitter. Many, like Cézanne, insist that a subject should sit 'as still as an apple'.

During our break for coffee, I was allowed to look at the canvas. I was astonished at the speed with which she had created the likeness. 'Don't forget', Judy said, 'I watched you for nearly an hour while you were giving your talk in Canberra. The likeness comes more quickly because of that.' Walking back to the hotel after the sitting I thought about her claim that a portrait painter's gaze is as searching as that of the therapist. What about the biographer? The analogy didn't quite work, I concluded, because the biographer doesn't normally come face to face with the subject. The dialogue with the dead has to be imagined.

Interviews were important for the last section of *The Boyds*. Of the four central figures, David Boyd was very much there, a living (and still painting) presence, and a close, passionately involved witness to his own childhood and to his parents. I had my own memories of Arthur and Guy, and a sense of their voices, their individual style. With Yvonne Boyd, only a few months after Arthur's death, and with Phyllis Boyd, twelve years after Guy's death, memories were so strong as almost to evoke presence. At its best, the interview, with its privileged, shared understanding, gives the biographer insights which no document can provide. Documents can't answer back:

they can't tell you where you are wrong. The written word doesn't give the tone of voice which yields the meaning, though with experience and a sufficient range of texts one can hope for a reliable interpretation. Could it be that the single vision of the portrait painter creates a closer likeness than a biography? But what if the sitter says: 'That's not me'? How does the painter defend her way of seeing? Whose life is it anyway, and whose face?

With these thoughts stirred by sitting for Judy Cassab, I find it hard to understand why I didn't then think of writing her life. The existence of her published diaries might have weighed against it. I would certainly have felt daunted by the difficulty of writing it in the lifetime of her husband. I had thought the diaries reticent about the marriage, and yet this was the aspect of the Cassab story which first interested me, as I compared her good fortune as an artist, wife and mother, with the frustrated talent of Georgiana McCrae. Jancsi Kämpfner, then very frail at ninety-five, came into the studio at each of my sittings, acknowledged my presence with a smile, gazed for a few moments at the portrait, but said nothing.

In 1998, in an exhibition of Cassab portraits at the Ervin Gallery in Sydney, I went to see Judy's version of me. There must have been several hundred guests at the opening, which included dozens of Judy's famous sitters: painters Margaret Olley, Charles Blackman among them, and public figures Margaret Whitlam, Michael Kirby. All of us, I am sure, were intent on seeing how our own likenesses appeared in one another's company.

While drinking champagne and chatting, or listening to the speeches, we all cast surreptitious glances on Judy's version of our selves.

I wasn't dismayed by my own portrait, though I remember saying uncertainly, 'I think I like it'. It had a quiet, reflective gaze; it was thoughtful, perhaps a bit remote. Was it Judy's idea of the biographer? I caught a momentary glimpse of a formidable great-aunt whom I had never thought I resembled. Judy had already sent me a photograph, and a letter in which she explained why I wasn't seen wearing the blue we had chosen. 'The blue didn't want to stay', she said. It showed through only as underpainting in a composition of silvery-gold. Her decision was rather like the writer's choice of tone of voice: if the tone is wrong, the story fails.

Soon after the exhibition of Cassab portraits I was once more absorbed in the Boyd family story. A recurring theme was that of the choices made by the Boyd women artists, who did not seek major careers. Similar choices were central to Judy Cassab's biography, but they did not immediately prompt me to write it. In a letter of sympathy written after her husband's death, I said that I thought of her marriage as a happy reversal of the fortunes of Georgiana McCrae in an earlier time. The happiness Judy Cassab and Jancsi Kämpfner shared was real, and remarkable in any time and place, but I knew nothing then of the underlying tensions, nor the price they paid for her career. *The Boyds* had been published for several months, during which I was vaguely aware of my need to be writing again, when the idea of a Cassab biography suddenly appeared as the right one, the only one possible for me.

Somehow, in a way I cannot easily remember or describe, a cluster of ideas and feelings came together. One day while searching for something else on my bookshelves (which defy Dewey or any other system) I noticed Judy Cassab's *Diaries*, and thought again about so much that was missing from that engaging but reticent account of her life. I hadn't been satisfied by my own review of the book; and seeing it again stirred a momentary regret. What was it that left me with a sense of unfinished business? Dissatisfaction with a newspaper review which has probably been written in a hurry, with limited space, is common enough. Too late for that one, will do better with the next: that would be my usual response. This time, questions lingered as I thought about Judy's early life. Because her prewar diaries were lost, it does not appear in the published *Diaries.* She had lost family and home in the Holocaust; she had been a refugee, a displaced person, a migrant in Sydney in 1951. Yet these themes are not fully developed in the *Diaries*, in which her Sydney painter's life takes precedence. While she was painting my portrait, the focus was always on me. Belatedly I thought of what I had missed in responding to her questions and not asking any of my own.

These random musings would have come to nothing except for two things, one personal, the other political. I wasn't writing anything, so there was a space to let until the next biographical subject came to mind. At the same time I was becoming acutely aware of the human dimension of Australian government policy on detention centres and shocked by its scant respect for the rights of refugees. A year after the *Tampa* affair, politicians were still talking self-righteously about queue-jumping. Television images of leaky boats sinking off the Australian coast brought memories of the homeless Vietnamese of an earlier time. Judy Cassab had spoken of the Vietnamese as 'the new Jews' whom no one wanted. She recalled her thankfulness when the Australian government accepted them as she and her family had been accepted. I have never thought that biographers should think of a cause and find a figure to exemplify it. If an individual's story opens out to embrace an idea, or express a moment in history, the biography will resonate, but such connections can't be forced. It seemed to me, as I thought about the new boat people and the squalid 'Pacific solution', that Judy Cassab's story re-entered my consciousness to say 'we have been here before'. Its effect, in showing the way to a new book, was rather like the sudden remembrance of Leon Edel and his 'string of beads' idea. Hence, my impulsive phone call of June 2002, and the series of questions I began to frame, even before her reply.

What was it that gave her the strength to survive persecution and exile, to start again in Sydney, and succeed in marriage and her painter's life? As I waited for Judy's response, I felt elated at the chance of a wonderful subject, even though I was intimidated at the prospect of entering such an unfamiliar world. Biographers need something to discover. There's no satisfaction in a rearrangement of facts, although a new way of seeing will light up a familiar space. The wish to understand what it was like to be a refugee, and the parallel impulse to tell a story for our times, would have been nothing without a central figure whose individuality had already caught my imagination. Judy Cassab's story had three intertwined themes: the artist, the wife and mother, and the refugee. Begin with an individual, Scott Fitzgerald said, and you will discover a type. Begin with a type, and you will have nothing. The Cassab story was about one woman. If reading her story brought readers to think about racism and a refugee's experience, well and good. But the biography would fail if it became a case study—and fail disastrously if it became a tract. Like a novelist, I write in order to understand, not to prove something.

The Cassab story had many surprises. In a letter to me, before we had our first interview, Judy said that we would need to talk about her home town. Although, like most biographers, I always go back to the beginnings, to retrieve childhood experience, I hadn't expected to meet such loss and longing as Judy invests in one place, the sub-Carpathian town, Beregszász, known after 1938 as Berehovo. She was born in Vienna, and spent the war years in Budapest, but her sense of exile is not bound up in either of those beautiful, war-damaged cities. It is all for Beregszász and her grandmother's house in the main street. Once part of the Austro-Hungarian Empire, now part of the Ukraine, the region to which this town belongs has a chequered history of occupations and 'liberations'.

In Judy's time, under the rule of the Czechoslovak Republic, between the two World Wars, Beregszász was peaceful and prosperous. Jewish families like hers had all the civic and personal rights which were being stripped with increasing brutality from the Jews of Austria, Germany and Hungary. A much-loved only child in a household of adults, Judy was praised and encouraged in every way. From the age of twelve, she was determined to be a professional artist. She thought of the world as a place of promise and delight. She looked forward to studying in Paris, seeing the great paintings she knew only from postcards, sketching in Montmartre with other artists, learning and living to the full.

When Hitler's war overturned her universe, Judy lost family and home. Ambitions were submerged in the traumas of persecution and war, although her need to paint remained strong. Only in the desperate year of 1944, when she masqueraded as a factory worker, using false identity papers, did she put her painting aside, because it was not in the part she was playing. After the siege of Budapest, at the end of 1944, and the Russian liberation of the city, she went back to Beregszász. All its buildings were intact, without the scars of bombing and gunfire she had known in Budapest, but empty of everything that had given it meaning. Her mother, grandmother, uncle and other family members had been taken to Auschwitz and murdered, along with nearly all of the town's 8000 Jews. Judy escaped their fate because she was living in Budapest, which the methodical exterminator Eichmann left to the last. First the country and the small towns, then the capital city; he did not have time to complete his task and so Judy and her husband survived.

As we talked in her quiet room in Double Bay, with the tape recorder running, I couldn't ask such banal questions as 'how did you feel when …?', nor were questions needed. The feeling was there in her tone of voice, and that could not easily be turned into words. If she had been in Auschwitz, I wouldn't have attempted to write her story. When she spoke about her mother, she did not use the words 'killed', 'murdered', or even 'died'. 'My mother was … taken away', she said, with a slight hesitation. And yet she was adamant in saying that 'these things have to be remembered'. When Roman Polanski's film *The Pianist* was shown in the Double Bay cinema in 2003 Judy did not flinch from seeing it, even though the experience of the central character so strongly reminded her of her husband's ordeals, hiding in 1944 Budapest as the last Jews were being hunted down.

We spent many hours in reconstructing Judy's childhood: the diary she kept from the age of twelve, her ambitions as an artist, her first commissions, when she painted the portraits of family friends in Beregszász, and used her fees to buy silk stockings. After initial hesitation she talked openly about her parents, who divorced when she was twelve. 'I never missed my father because I never had him', she said firmly, as she stressed the role of her mother's brothers in supplying paternal love. I was puzzled to find that she had very few memories of Vienna, which she left as a nine-year-old, and almost nothing to say about three years in a Budapest boarding house, in straitened circumstances, before her parents separated and she and her mother went to live in Beregszász. Life began in Beregszász, it seemed, and her memories from the age of twelve were vivid and detailed.

Writing about those years, I suggested that such a black-out of memory might be due to childhood trauma. Judy had spoken of her mother's depression as a fact of life in the Beregszász years. Was this illness more acute in the Budapest boarding house? A sensitive only child, having lost her father in the separation, with her mother unable to give security, might have obliterated the period from memory. From this, I thought, might stem Judy's total identification with Beregszász, where, at twelve years old, she was seemingly re-born as painter, diarist, high-achieving schoolgirl, and beloved, sheltered child in her grandmother's house.

Whether Judy believed my hypothesis I don't know. She read every word of the completed book before publication but neither assented to nor denied my reading of this period. Speaking of her desolation on the post-war return to the deserted town, she said that her whole childhood had been taken away, 'burnt in the ovens of Auschwitz'. After that one visit in March 1945 she never returned to Beregszász. It soon became inaccessible, under Soviet rule, but even if it had been possible to go back she would not have done so. There was nothing left of her past.

The series of interviews continued with Judy's account of having fallen in love, just after her graduation from high school, with Jancsi Kämpfner, a man twice her age; his decision to defer marriage so that she could have a free year as an art student in Prague; and the subsequent reversal of that decision when Hitler's troops invaded the Czech Republic in March 1938. Having made her way home, Judy married Jancsi to the sound of gunfire, as the Czechs put up sporadic resistance to the re-defined national boundaries. I asked Judy what it was in Jancsi Kämpfner that made her so sure of her decision to marry. She hesitated, while the tape ran on. Then she crossed the room and held out a framed photograph of her husband, taken at the time of their marriage. 'There!' she said, as if that settled it. And it did, not so much because of the responsiveness and strength of the pictured face, but because of her certainty. 'If I would have my life over again I would still be an artist. And I would marry the same man,' she said more than once.

Biographer's time is not calendar time. Although I planned the first half-dozen sessions so as to move chronologically through the years from the 1920s to the mid-1940s, we would circle back many times to Beregszász and wartime Budapest. Judy's 'sittings' with me were structured in exactly the same way as my portrait sittings with her had been, six years earlier. We observed the rituals of coffee and little sugared biscuits at half time, and except that we were in Judy's sitting room instead of the studio, it was almost the same kind of exchange. It was orderly and contained, like the sittings, but on my part there was a far more intense concentration than I had needed, or felt, as a portrait subject.

On Judy's part, there was inevitably a powerful stirring of emotions as she revisited her past. Later, I watched the videotape of her interview with Shirley Eisenberg for the Survivors of the Shoah Visual History program which was recorded for the Spielberg Foundation in 1995. By then, my own interviews had taken her story through the experiences of postwar displacement, arrival in 1950s Sydney, her first win in the Archibald Prize, and as I looked though her press cutting album I saw a poised and elegant woman in her new world.

To circle back from postwar Sydney to the horrors of the 1940s was a reminder, if I needed it, that the past is never left behind. An old photograph album held a small, faded photograph of a group of factory workers. Judy, aged twenty-four, is there, in her masquerade on false papers in Budapest in 1944. Wearing the shapeless smock that was the workers' uniform, smoking a cigarette, she looks blankly at the camera. It made a poignant contrast with the radiant child in an earlier photograph, twelve-year-old Judy in the garden of her grandmother's house in Beregszász.

When I first thought of the Cassab biography, I assumed that it would involve many weeks in libraries.

It was a relief to know that the Cassab diaries, from which only a selection had been published, were held by the National Library of Australia, a good place to work, as I knew very well from my Boyd research. On my first exploratory visit to the library I was elated by the range and quality of the material, but daunted too. There was so much more than I had bargained for that I began to think of renting a flat in Canberra for three or four months, which would be less expensive than comings and goings from Melbourne. I came home from the first session in Canberra with a notebook crammed with pencilled entries, knowing that I would get on faster with a lap-top, but even with that advance in method, it would be a long haul.

The Library holds ten folio-size typed volumes. Each of them, in a rough estimate, must comprise three or four hundred pages, at five hundred words per page. The alarming total might be as much as two million words. Two more volumes had been typed and would be added to the archive. And meanwhile Judy, my living subject, was continuing her daily entries. Having often mourned the destruction of many years of Georgiana McCrae's diaries, and regretted the taciturn style of Emma à Beckett's entries, it looked as if I might now be overwhelmed by the Cassab riches. How long would it take me to read them in Canberra and take notes?

Although my biography would show only a fraction of the Cassab material, the whole record of diary entries, from 1944 to 2002, would have to be explored, and much of it transcribed. There would be other material: letters, notebooks, newspaper cuttings, videotapes, photograph albums. There would be portfolios of sketches, racks and stacks of paintings, framed and unframed, in studio and garage as well as those in galleries; more than fifty years of the life work of a dedicated, prolific artist. 'All my life', Judy said, 'I put something on a page or on canvas. If I don't, I feel as though I wouldn't have lived that day. That's me.'

I never quite confronted the inexorable mathematics of my situation. I was too deeply involved in the project to think of withdrawing; and to count the pages and estimate my rate of reading was hardly worth the time and trouble. Others have worked with much larger archives, more complex and widely scattered papers. I thought of British biographer Claire Tomalin, whose life of Pepys was then in progress. How was she dealing with that immense daily chronicle? But at least she knew its limits. I knew that as fast as I wrote, Judy would be writing too. You cannot catch up with a living subject.

While I was still considering ways and means, Judy eased matters immeasurably by offering her own set of diaries, duplicates of those she had given the National Library. The first years had been translated from the Hungarian by Judy herself so that her two sons could read them. After that, having made herself much more fluent by the exercise of translation, she began to write in English. For the next two years, while the biography progressed, I had Judy's twelve bound folio-size volumes in my study, accessible by day or night, whenever I wanted to explore, revisit, or just check a date. She also lent me her scrapbooks of reviews, interviews and other newspaper cuttings that charted her painting career in Sydney. It was a tremendous gift, which must have shortened my research time by a year or more, and saved me air fares and hotel bills in Canberra, as well as personal wear and tear. When I visited Vienna, Prague and Budapest in 2004, there was nothing I could do in libraries, and almost no one to meet. Even if I had been able to read or speak Hungarian, there were no documented family sources. The war had seen to that. Nevertheless, the settings of Judy's early life, the landscapes and art galleries, the paintings she knew, even the coffee houses where she met her friends—all these helped immensely. To see the scars of battle on the ramparts of Buda, and to look down at the Danube bridges, now rebuilt, which the retreating Germans destroyed, told me more than many printed texts could do.

Writing the biography of a living subject brings some surprising gifts. One of these was to watch Judy Cassab in her monthly drawing group, with artist friends Margaret Woodward and Charles Blackman. The two-hour session showed Judy, the social being who greeted us all with characteristic warmth, lose herself in absolute concentration on Marina, the nude model, and on the free, flowing line of her sketch. The work done, the hospitable Judy re-awakened to preside over the ritual of strong coffee, cherry strudel and conversation.

Judy's social self, so charming, so attuned to those she meets, could have been a barrier to understanding. Someone who is shy and awkward may be easier to read. I had two advantages. One was the directness with which she meets any question. Provided I had the courage to ask, she would not hold back. Moreover, the diaries held her own self-scrutiny. As wife and mother she felt that she often failed, and her reflections are probably more severe than mine would have been. Quoting her own appraisal of the tensions in her marriage, and her re-creation of some stormy moments, brought her personality into sharp relief, saving the biography from being too distant, or too polite and tentative.

I don't think that many biographers have the experience of reading themselves as a part of the life they are writing. In an uncanny circling movement, I read Judy's diary entry for 14 May 2001, to find my letter of sympathy on her husband's death, which she had transcribed in full. In the next volume, there was her record of my phone call to her on 17 June 2002. And her entry for that day:

> Out of the blue a call from Brenda Niall from Melbourne. It must be a year we haven't been in touch. I read glowing reports in the papers about her new book. She wrote about the Boyds. She wants her next book to be about me. 'Brenda, I'm honoured, I feel flattered. But my diary …' 'I'd like MY version of your life. Starting with the first twenty-three years you have not written about in the diary. I'd come over

for interviews.' An exciting new turn, by a serious writer.

Reading this entry was disconcerting: a reminder that just as she had become part of my life, Judy was making me part of hers. Her way of recording my words, however, was reassuring. I had said that her diary was a self-portrait, while my biography would be a portrait. Did I say 'MY version' so emphatically? At any rate, Judy understood from the first that, just as her portraits were her own, no matter on whose walls they hung, this would be my book.

One interview to remember. One day in Sydney, while I was visiting and interviewing Judy, I needed to have my hair cut; and thought I would go to Judy's hairdresser. While Louis of Double Bay was busy with the scissors, I asked him about his famous client. He told me a wonderful story. He had suggested to Judy that it was time to have a new hairstyle. She agreed, saying 'It's your hair, Louis, I only wear it'.

She never said to me: 'It's your life, Brenda. I only live it.' But she did say, more than once, 'You are the writer. It's your book.' She always thought of the biography, as she thinks of a portrait, as having a life of its own; and as an interpretation for which the writer must be allowed to take responsibility. 'My sitters don't tell me how to paint', she said; and she didn't try to direct my interviews. And when she read the final typescript, slowly and carefully, over two weeks, sending her responses by e-mail as

I waited in suspense, she made a few corrections of fact but didn't ask for any changes.

Soon after the book was published, I was a guest at the Writers' Week of the Brisbane Festival. After I'd talked about the Cassab book, there were a few questions, none of them very searching. Then it was time to sign copies. A woman in her eighties, with a European accent, came over to the booksellers' table. She had been at my talk and she now put a question she hadn't felt able to ask in public. She said: 'Do you really think that a book like yours, or any book, can help anyone to understand the Holocaust?' It wasn't a hostile question; she took my hand and held it gently as she spoke, in case I might be offended. Then she said: 'I was there—I was in the camps, and I still don't understand it'.

Rather lamely, I said that any understanding, however small, might help people like me, and nearly all my readers, who knew so little. I wouldn't claim to have lit even the smallest candle. At most, perhaps it could be a momentary scrape and flare of a match, struck in an immense darkness. Even so, the attempt to strike that match—to cross that boundary—seems worth doing. Nothing will come of nothing.

10

Time Capsule: Finding Father Hackett

One sunny autumn day in 2005 I walked through Boroondara cemetery in Kew, looking for the grave of William Hackett, who was born in Ireland in 1878 and died in Melbourne in 1954, after thirty years of work in the Australian province of the Jesuit order. Idly pondering Hackett's life as a possible, though unlikely, biographical subject, I was curious to see what kind of monument he had in this crowded, quiet place. I had almost decided that it would be folly to accept an invitation to write William Hackett's life, but I hadn't quite put the idea aside. Biographies of priests are seldom written, and for good reason. The vows of poverty, chastity and obedience rule out much that is common to human experience. Hidden lives may have rich inner drama, but they don't easily sustain a narrative. Members of the Jesuit order, by custom and the commitment of their rule, travel light, ready to go where they are needed, at short notice. The chances of their accumulating private papers, at least in Hackett's time, are small. A life of a priest who died fifty years ago would not tempt any publisher. And yet, because for me Hackett's memory was strong, his personality engaging and complex, it tempted me.

What was there in Hackett's life that might sustain a biography? This charming, quirky individualist was also a representative of an important moment in Irish–Australian history. Men who left Ireland in the 1920s, as Hackett did, left a nation torn apart by political passions. Whatever their attitudes to the nationalist movement, they could not escape the emotional turmoil of the Easter Rising of 1916, when in Yeats' phrase, 'a terrible beauty' was born. Many who grew up in 1930s and 1940s Kew, as I did, remembered Hackett as Rector of Xavier and heard the legends about his Irish Republican connections. Was it true that his superiors hastily despatched him to Australia in 1922 because he was dangerously close to the Republican leaders in time of civil war? To be sent to Melbourne did not mean forgetting the emotions of that time, not while that other Irishman, Archbishop Daniel Mannix, ruled from Raheen. It was common knowledge that Hackett became one of Mannix's closest friends. Yet, I reflected, that fact didn't necessarily make him more interesting.

In the shadow of the dominant Mannix, whose inscrutable public persona has defied half a dozen biographers, William Hackett might be obscured.

Not much here, I thought, as I walked on the cracked, uneven pathways towards the Jesuit plots. Rose bushes in long lines mark the places where the ashes of the recently dead are buried. Next come the Italian family graves, lavish with gold lettering, endearments, plastic flowers in bright colours, cameo photographs of the dead, gilt-framed. In the distance I can see the little Gothic chapel built by the Cussen family for their son who died young. The extravaganza of the cemetery, the Springthorpe Memorial, outdoes all others, with the weeping angel above the grave of a mother who died in childbirth, leaving a husband so distracted with grief and guilt that her memorial in marble became an obsession.

There are no such signs of mourning among the Jesuit graves. Of all the memorials to the dead in Boroondara, which stretch back over one hundred and fifty years, these are perhaps the most austere. It is not that they look neglected, like some where weeds grow in the cracks of marble slabs, or where broken headstones tilt at eccentric angles. They are built so as to need no care. A large rectangular plot, rimmed with black or dark grey marble, is covered in grey-white pebbles, through which no weeds grow. There are four Jesuit plots, all much the same. I find the one I want, with the early and mid-twentieth century graves. In the centre, below a grey stone Celtic cross, the names of twenty-four Jesuits are inscribed. Here is the name of William Hackett, and the dates 1878–1954. Here too is his contemporary Jeremiah Murphy, former Rector of Newman College. Nothing to show that both men came from Kilkenny, nor that both of them arrived in Melbourne in the early 1920s. Nothing of their Irish past. No commemoration of their work, or the place in Melbourne life won by these two remarkable men. 'Patres et Fratres', the priests and brothers of the Jesuit order are equal here, under the collective AMDG inscription: For the Greater Glory of God.

No birthplace is set down, nor is there any place for 'beloved son …' It was part of the Jesuit culture of Hackett's time to see the order as the only family. The graves were not important. Death opened the door to resurrection. There was nothing to mourn. The community would have sung their brother to heaven and whatever their private feelings of loss, gone on with their work. There would be few if any possessions. If there were private papers, they would normally be burned unread. The inevitable clerical black overcoat might be thriftily passed on to another priest of more or less the same size. A wrist watch, a pipe and tobacco pouch might well be the most personal items to be disposed of.

Walking back to the street, crunching the brittle autumn leaves underfoot, I felt sure that the life of William Hackett could only be reconstructed from public sources, and from whatever living testimony I could find. No hope of personal papers, I thought, but such a vivid personality would have left his impression, as he did on me, from my early childhood in 1930s Kew. The upper windows in our house in Studley Park Road looked across to the domed chapel of Xavier College, where Hackett spent many years. Boys on their way home from school, my brothers' friends, often dropped in; and so did some of the priests, to see my father.

Of those Jesuit visitors, it was restless, sociable William Hackett who came most often, and whom I remember with most affection. Spare, quick-moving, with pink cheeks, blue eyes bright behind steel-framed spectacles, he had the invaluable quality of being exactly the same to children as to adults, to women as to men. He didn't talk down to us, nor did he censor his conversation. 'I am summoned to Portsea', he would say, describing the rigours of his annual holiday in attendance on Archbishop Mannix. The Archbishop was then in his mid-eighties; he did not take more than a very short stroll in the garden, and while the sea beckoned to adventurous Hackett (still active in his early seventies) there was no chance of swimming or boating. 'I am the court jester', he said. It was his task to talk to the old man during the long summer afternoons. The holidays were a mixture of the splendid and the spartan. The crystal and silver were brought from Raheen; but good cooking meant nothing to Dr Mannix. 'That man could live on a caraway seed', Hackett said. To spend the summer months in his company was a great honour ('though no one else wants it') and he revered the old man, but the six weeks passed slowly.

At our house for dinner, or calling in on impulse during the evening, Hackett would take an armchair by the study fire and talk happily about books, people, places, ideas, enjoying a good cigar, scarcely noticing that the baby of our family, not yet walking, was expertly untying his shoelaces. I looked forward to his visits, for more than one reason. My father, who didn't smoke cigars, kept a box of Havanas almost exclusively for Hackett. When the last one was consumed, the decorative box with its smoothly sliding lid would make a perfect pencil case. I wished that Father Hackett would take a second cigar, but he never did. Later, when I had moved on from coveting the cigar box, I still enjoyed Hackett's visits.

I was impressed when he brought us a copy of a new book by his brother Francis, a founding editor of the *New Republic,* who lived in Chicago. Francis Hackett's *Henry VIII*, a bestseller in the 1930s, must have been one of the first biographies I read. Even more impressive was the fact that Father Hackett had been at boarding school with James Joyce, at Clongowes Wood College. He knew the scenes and some of the people whose fictional versions appear in *Portrait of the Artist as a Young Man*. 'A strange boy, a very strange boy', Father Hackett said, and regrettably left it at that. His great passion was his perpetually under-funded Central Catholic Library; and one of his recurring themes was the difficulty of finding patrons. He had great hopes of the Cody family, who gave so generously to Xavier, and he never quite gave up on John Wren, though conceding that books meant nothing to the man who had made his millions from the gambling industry. Then there was a Mrs Nicholas, whose family owned the Aspro patent, who was thinking of becoming a Catholic. Why couldn't these people take more interest in the Library?

There was a Micawber-like optimism about Hackett that went with an eager responsiveness to experience, and a wide-ranging intellectual curiosity. His disdain for practical matters, including the need to balance a budget, must have made him an exasperating colleague. At Xavier he was well known as a maverick Rector who infuriated old boys and mothers' committee members for his insouciant attitude to such orthodoxies as public school sports and the need to 'get on in life'. Yet it was hard to be in his presence without feeling that the world was full of wonderful possibilities. As, indeed, was the next world. 'It will be so *interesting* to find out', he said cheerfully, 'what God has in mind for us'.

My memories are those of the charming old man in his well-worn clerical black, warming himself at our fireside before being driven back to his chilly room at Xavier. Fifty years after his death, can I hope to evoke the young Hackett? There are dozens of stories about him, many of which might be apocryphal. Was it true that Hackett had tried to arrange a meeting to reconcile de Valera and Michael Collins during the first months of the Irish Civil War? It was said that years afterwards he still wept for the dead of Easter 1916, including his friend Padraig Pearse, and for Erskine Childers, who was executed in 1922.

Had he hidden ammunition for the Republicans during the Civil War, and risked arrest from the Free State army? And defied the Irish bishops by hearing confessions and giving absolution to Republicans who took de Valera's side against Collins and the Free State? Did Michael Collins really say, while England's Black and Tans were burning Irish cottages, that Hackett was worth five hundred men in arms? And if any or all of these stories were true, what effect would Hackett's Irish nationalism have had on the Australian scene of his later life? In the ever-present tensions between the Catholic Church and the secular society, from Mannix and the Irish question to the Australian Labor Party and Santamaria's Movement, did Hackett play a decisive role? Or was he, as he described himself, no more than Mannix's 'court jester'?

Pondering these questions—almost certainly unanswerable—I was interested enough to make an appointment with the Jesuit archivist, Michael Head SJ. Depending on what had survived in the records, I might be able to write something for the Eldon Hogan Trust, whose invitation started it all. An unusual bequest from Eldon Hogan, a very unusual Old Xaverian, empowered his trustee to support works of cultural history relating to the Jesuit order in Melbourne. When the invitation came, I had just completed my biography of Judy Cassab. This portrait of an artist, set against a background of European politics, had made me think about religious and racial divisions, and the impact of Europe's tragedies on an immigrant society like Australia. In spite of my Irish Catholic background I had never taken much interest in the Irish question. With time to spare while I thought about a new biography, I could perhaps give a few months to William Hackett. In this mood of qualified scepticism I kept my appointment in the Jesuit archives in Hawthorn, where I spent an astonishing morning.

In the basement archive, purpose-built, with a concrete floor, row after row of steel shelving holds hundreds of boxes. Each box, and sometimes more than one, holds the record of a Jesuit's life in Australia. They are shelved according to the date of death, so that a long life may sit beside one that was cut short early: an old priest from Ireland beside an Australian who died young. Here among those who departed in 1954 is William Hackett who, at the age of seventy-six, was knocked down by a taxi as he crossed busy Cotham Road, Kew, one winter evening after giving Benediction at Genazzano Convent. Black coat, black umbrella, invisible to the driver, impetuous, quick-moving as always, he was critically injured. 'I've had a bit of an upset', he told a visitor who saw him in hospital. Close to death, a few days later, he whispered, 'I never thought I'd have a taxi to take me to heaven'.

It's not surprising, given Hackett's gift for friendship and for a witty phrase in any circumstances, that his death is so well remembered, even half a century later. But I was amazed to discover that Hackett's beginnings are on record, as if waiting for a biographer. Letters home to his parents in Kilkenny from twelve-year-old William at boarding school in 1890; letters from seminaries in Ireland, France and Holland, letters from Dublin and Limerick during Ireland's troubles of the 1920s; they are all here, as are his letters from 1940s and 1950s Melbourne to his sister, novelist and playwright Florence Hackett.

This is not what I was led to expect. 'When a Jesuit dies', I had been told, 'someone will come in next day with a wheelie-bin, clear out the room and take the papers to the incinerator'. Or, let's hope, to the shredder. The archive, professionally maintained, disproves that rule. Clearly, history is important. But a private record, with family papers going back to a late-nineteenth-century Irish childhood, is a rare find. Michael Head explains. Soon after Father Hackett's death, a young Jesuit, Doug Boyd, had the idea of writing the life of a man whom he admired greatly. Permission was given—though not the spare time needed for the task—and Boyd wrote to the last surviving Hackett in Kilkenny, asking for family papers. Delighted at the idea of her brother's life being remembered, Florence Hackett sent a large collection of papers and photographs which might well have made a bonfire in Kilkenny when she died there a few years later. Doug Boyd never wrote the biography. He died in 1995, and the archive has never been fully explored, although some researchers have dipped into it for specific purposes.

By good fortune, too, Hackett proved to be a hoarder of correspondence during his thirty years in Australia. As the director of the Central Catholic Library in

Melbourne from 1923 until his death in 1954, he had a permanent address, so that in spite of many transfers, at short notice, from schools to parishes and back again, he never had to disturb his papers.

There were eight Hackett boxes, each one crammed full of manila folders. Writing about the Boyds and Georgiana McCrae I had often explored family papers, so the surge of excitement was not new. Yet there was a difference. The Boyd and McCrae papers were scattered, in libraries, in private hands, in Scotland, in the UK, as well as Australia; and as I visited each site of exploration I often had to make quick decisions as to what to read then and there, whether I should ask to borrow or photocopy, and how to divide my time between interviews and documentary research. The Hackett archive could be explored at my own pace. Having been almost undisturbed for fifty years, it would be here next week, next month, next year. I could have the luxury of beginning at the beginning, rather than zigzagging through a life in haphazard time sequence. In fact, I was tempted by the personal connection and began at the end.

The sequence of almost weekly letters to Hackett's sister Florence in the 1940s and early 1950s takes me back to Kew Hill and our own fireside. It was an uncanny moment to unfold a letter of 1952, and to read Hackett's words of distress at my father's death. 'This was a great blow. He was one of my best friends as well as my doctor.' His funeral was 'splendid and representative—unusual even for Melbourne'.[1]

Three months later Hackett is shocked and saddened by the death of Arthur Niall, also a close friend. Arthur found the old house in Brighton that became Xavier's bayside preparatory school, and negotiated with the owners on Hackett's behalf. For today's Xavier historians, that's a mystery solved. Arthur must have been the anonymous (and some thought reckless) 'silver-tongued persuader' referred to by Hackett when the purchase was announced. Late in the same year Hackett writes of his pleasure in my sister Philippa's engagement to 'an exceedingly nice lad, Maurice Ryan' whom he taught at Xavier before the war. And in his last letter, just before the accident, 'What will the Ryans call their baby?' Hackett wonders.

Other households, other visits, bring back familiar names. Our neighbours the Codys are there. Mat Cody is soon to visit Kilkenny. 'Do find him an Irish wife', Hackett urges. The letters show Hackett's warmth and his capacity to enter into the family life of his friends, as well as his enduring affection for his sister, the youngest of his large family, whom he hadn't seen since 1922, and would never see again. 'My dearest Flo', the letters begin. They end with 'much love from Willie'. Writing freely and openly, he could never have imagined that these airletters—flimsies, as he calls them—would be kept, sent back from Ireland to Australia, and read more than half a century after his death by one of the Studley Park children—the one who wanted his cigar box for a pencil case. Airletters, I discover, are extravagances at sevenpence each. After paying seven and sevenpence for train and tram fares out of his allowance of ten shillings a week, Hackett has to coax extra stamps and airletters from his superior. He can never afford cigars, which are the one indulgence of a committed total abstainer from alcohol. They come now and then as a gift from one of his brothers in the United States, or in the houses of friends like his doctor, Frank Niall. Should my father have known better? It seems not: the findings on smoking will not be known for some years. It's hard to move on from these personal glimpses and connections but they are not enough to make a biography.

If there is a book here, much of its interest will come from Hackett's life in Ireland, from his 1880s childhood to the Easter Rising and the Civil War. Settling into a weekly routine in the Jesuit archives, enjoying good talk at hospitable morning teas, I look through the folders of letters from Irish friends. I read a series from the family of Erskine Childers, author of *The Riddle of the Sands,* the 'damned Englishman', mistrusted by some Irishmen and hated by Churchill. Childers espoused the Irish Republican cause and was executed by Irish Free Staters in 1922. I find that Trinity College, Dublin, holds some Childers papers. And, yes, they have some Hackett letters, I find after an exchange of e-mails. Reading Mollie Childers' account of the night before the execution, when she was not allowed to see her husband, I feel certain that she would have kept Hackett's reply. And, sure enough, she did. I retrieve two letters from Trinity College which show a Hackett quite unlike the buoyant old man I knew. Writing of Childers' death, he struggles with the powerful emotions of Ireland's saddest years, felt even more strongly because of his own exile in Australia:

> My grief is increased by the fact that I am so far away & I cannot go over to Number 12 & let you have my sympathy. It is hard to be away now. Very hard. All the more because it looks like cowardice. [Erskine's] supreme sacrifice cannot—will not be lost. I say this with a physical catching at my heart, for I have said it so often as my friends have dropped away one by one—Pierce McCann & Michael O'Callaghan & now Erskine—that one almost doubts the truth of the formula but I do not doubt.
>
> I think Erskine the greatest man I have met—save the chief [de Valera]. I want you to feel that I enter fully into your immeasurable loss. I look upon yesterday's work as the worst in Ireland in my lifetime. I pray there will be no reprisals.[2]

Before I explored the Hackett papers, I saw the project in general terms as a means of discovering what kind of psychological baggage the Irish Jesuits brought to Australia in the 1920s. That is still the aim, but it became a much more personal quest. The word 'baggage' soon took a literal meaning. The papers Hackett nonchalantly brought from Ireland include copies of an illegal newsheet that documented the atrocities committed by the British. Possession of these newsheets, classed as seditious literature ('likely to incite unlawful behaviour') was matter for a court martial and a two-year sentence in an English gaol. Terence McSwiney, mayor of Cork, arrested for possession of material like this, died in Brixton prison in 1920 after seventy-four days on hunger strike.[3] Another item in Hackett's luggage, equally likely to incite unlawful behaviour in 1920, was a small envelope of photographs, faded now but still eloquent. He had escorted a group of English Quakers to see the work of the Black and Tans, and the photographs were his own. The appalling scene included a charred body, which Hackett described but could not bring himself to photograph. The Quakers, he said, were ashamed of their countrymen.

Every discovery shifts the biographer's boundaries. Now that I know how closely Hackett was involved in Ireland's struggle for independence from Britain, and in the fratricidal divisions of the Civil War, I want to understand his adjustment to life in Australia. Serenity is not quite the word for Hackett, but his faith and his religious vocation were unshaken. His zest for life seemed never to fail. Witty, sometimes sharp, never malicious, he showed no trace of bitterness. 'In the [Jesuit] order one is always at home', he wrote. There was talk of his visiting Ireland with Archbishop Mannix, but he was ambivalent about the idea. He would have liked to see Ireland again, but quietly, without the 'hullabaloo' that would attend the great man. Australia was where God wanted him to work. He accepted that without question.

This brings another question: what did Hackett contribute to the Irish nationalism of Archbishop Mannix, his friend of many years? Mannix left Ireland in 1913. He had none of Hackett's painful eyewitness experiences, nor the close friendships with the men of 1916 and the hunger strikers who died in British gaols in the early 1920s. I read Hackett's amusing accounts, in letters to 'dearest Flo' of his weekly visits to Archbishop Mannix, and their annual holiday at Queenscliff and later at Portsea. Here, at last, is the personal viewpoint on Mannix that I missed so many years ago when interviewing the Archbishop for the Santamaria biography. Here is Hackett's attempt to bring the Governor of Victoria, Lord Somers, to Raheen for a chat. Mannix refuses. Hackett takes Somers to the Dandenongs for a very long walk and shows him how to boil the billy. How does a friendship with the King's representative fit in with Hackett's Irish Republicanism?

More questions and puzzles remain: there is much work still to be done on the Australian years, on Xavier College and the Central Catholic Library. Late in his life Hackett was appointed chaplain to the National Secretariat of Catholic Action: 'duties light, salary nil', he said. Did he try to mend fences between the *Catholic Worker* intellectuals whom his Library had nurtured and Santamaria's Movement, which he would certainly have supported? Hackett visited the Wren family during their case for criminal libel against Frank Hardy, author of *Power Without Glory*. Indignant on Mrs Wren's behalf, he is astonished by her calm.

I mustn't linger yet in the late period of Hackett's life, beguiling though it is to meet my childhood period over again and to find new insights on Mannix. I need to go back to beginnings. Feeling like an archaeologist on the edge of a promising dig, I choose the box labelled Family and Irish Letters, and settle in. In the archivist's sequence this is Box 4. It follows boxes of political pamphlets, sermons, and personal notes made during spiritual retreats. But before I come closer to William Hackett, political activist, priest and scrutineer of his soul's adventures, I want to place the young Willie, with his parents, brothers and sisters in 1880s Ireland.

And so I open Box 4, which holds twelve-year-old Willie Hackett's letters home from Clongowes Wood College to 'dearest Pappie and Mud', as he calls his parents. At home that evening I turn to Google, and idly type in Hackett Kilkenny, expecting nothing. But there they are: the family and their house, which is now a 'boutique hotel', the Kilkenny Hibernian. Through the Kilkenny Archeological Society website I find two Kilkenny historians. Frank McEvoy remembers Florence Hackett as vividly as I remember her brother. Mary Flood has written a thesis on the biographer Francis Hackett. I look forward to almost nightly news from Kilkenny on e-mail, as well as documents and photographs in the post, as they reply to my questions. Our lively ongoing conversation is a new experience for me in long-distance biographical research. I hear stories of the Kilkenny Hacketts, not least the father of the family, Dr John Byrne Hackett, a close friend and public supporter of the doomed leader Charles Stewart Parnell. It's evident that the young Willie grew up at the centre of Irish nationalist politics. As a young priest he rebuked his brothers for radicalism, but the executions of Easter 1916 shocked him into commitment. Against all probability, I can see that a full-scale Hackett biography is feasible. It is historically important, for its Irish background and its Irish–Australian religious and political reverberations. And because it touches my own past, stirring memories of childhood and the Kew Hill that I remember, it is irresistible.

Afterword

'Never say you know the last word about any human heart.' Henry James, who disliked biography, and did his best to frustrate the writing of his own life, reminds us of the limits of understanding another's experience, or even our own. Now that I have looked back at my half-dozen biographical works, one of them still in the making, I find myself wanting to rewrite them all. No great alterations, just a touch here and there, with an addition, perhaps, of a story I heard after finishing the book, a better phrase in place of one that simplifies, a shift in emphasis that allows another aspect of personality to be more clearly seen. That doesn't mean I disown my books, still less that I feel daunted by the biographical adventure. Just as any ordinary human relationship brings surprises and rethinkings, so does the relation between biographer and subject. Times change, as I have changed. Thirty years ago, transfixed by the riches of the Edith Wharton papers at Yale, but unsure of myself and intimidated by distance, I let a chance go by. Now, as I begin to interpret the life of William Hackett, whose archive is almost on my doorstep, but whose early life touches much of the troubled history of modern Ireland, I take this latest chance with more confidence, accepting uncertainty as part of the enterprise.

When I began to write *Life Class* I didn't expect my own life to push its way as far in as it has done, but I thought it should be there. Increasingly aware of the biographer's role in selecting and shaping, I wanted to take a backward glance at my late, uncertain start as an academic and a writer of other people's lives. And so, inevitably, given a biographer's habit of mind, I went back to beginnings. I seldom keep old papers, except by accident. I don't possess that romantic biographer's dream, the trunk in the attic. More prosaically, I have a trunk in my garden shed which holds a miscellany of old letters, school reports, lecture notes, income tax returns, photographs. Expelled from my study but not quite deserving the shredder, the contents of the trunk is a lucky dip, full of things I had forgotten, possibilities of lives I didn't lead. Could I have been a serious scholar? My Anglo-Saxon and Middle English notes are better than I'd expected. Whatever happened to my interest in medieval drama? Did I really read all those eighteenth-century novels, or was the essay on Fielding and Richardson, as I rather suspect, a bluff? If I had left for England to study in 1953, as planned, I might now be leading a quite different life. Happier than now? Perhaps, perhaps not. Staying at home worked out pretty well in the end. There were some hard lessons and some bleak years, and if I hadn't eventually found my way, I would probably now feel resentful or self-reproachful. As it is, I weigh the good things: the gifts of love, friendship and creative work, and find plenty of reasons for rejoicing.

Biographers can cheat, or deceive themselves with photographs. It's tempting to find auguries in those old Kodaks, even though the context is uncertain. Nevertheless, I rummage among the papers in search of some early images of myself. I find the ten-year-old on her pony, confidently facing the camera in Norah of Billabong style. Next, at eighteen, in a cheerful group on Mount Martha beach, the sun in my eyes. Nothing prophetic here.

But the earliest picture: that's the one to interest a biographer. In a studio portrait, one of a set of four, taken when I was about two years old, I am looking down with intense concentration at an alphabet block, almost frowning, as if I really need to know the meaning of the letter Z. The other three photographs which, in the fashion of the 1930s, were framed together as a sequence, include one holding a doll and one with a direct gaze, smiling for the camera. I remember the ritual of being held up by my father to look at the whole set, which hung on my parents' bedroom wall, and being asked as he pointed at each one: 'Who's that?' 'Me!' I claimed them all, delighted at the four separate pictured selves which were all my own. Who gave me the alphabet block to hold? The photographer, perhaps, or my parents. As a means of making a very young child keep still for the camera, it worked. What's more, the alphabet block was a beginning. The gift of words has lasted me well.

Some years after my retirement from university teaching, just back from overseas travel for *The Boyds*, I met a neighbour who asked a few questions about my career. She commented, in a tone of some surprise, 'You've had quite an interesting life, haven't you?' I didn't much like the past tense, so I replied with just a touch of asperity. 'I am still having it.'

Notes

Preface

1 Richard Holmes, *Sidetracks, Explorations of a Romantic Biographer*, HarperCollins, London, 2000, p. 198.
2 Michael Holroyd, *Basil Street Blues*, Little, Brown, London, 1999, p. 3.
3 Erik Erikson,'On the Nature of Psycho-Historical Evidence: in Search of Gandhi', *Daedalus*, 97, 1968, p. 713.

1 On Kew Hill

1 Kevin Gorman, 'The Gorman Family: Seven Generations in Australia', *The Author*, 1997, ch. 5, *passim*.
2 Donald Horne, *The Education of Young Donald*, Penguin Books, Ringwood, rev. ed. 1988, p. 20.
3 Inga Clendinnen, *Tiger's Eye: a Memoir*, Text Publishing, Melbourne, 2000, p. 152.

2 First Lessons

1 Janet McCalman, *Journeyings: the Biography of a Middle-Class Generation 1920–1990*, Melbourne University Press, Carlton, 1993, p. 129.

3 Interviewing the Archbishop

1 A phrase used of Dr Mannix by William Hackett SJ. Hackett Papers, Jesuit Archives, Hawthorn, Victoria.
2 BA Santamaria, 'Reflections on the White Australia Policy', *Twentieth Century*, 13, Winter 1959, pp. 329–42.
3 The Movement was the abbreviated name of the Catholic Social Studies Movement, which from 1945 had been engaged in wide-ranging attempts to educate Catholics in social thought, and to combat communist influence in the trade unions. Its social thinking (on co-operative ownership and shareholding by workers, decentralisation, development of rural life, increased migration) was often seen as utopian. In organising Catholic trade union members to take an active part in union affairs, matching communist efforts at meetings and in elections, the CSSM had remarkable success, though hardly the 'control' that it was credited with, as the events of 1954 were to prove.

4 Among many accounts of the sequence of events, see John Douglas Pringle, *Australian Accent*, Chatto and Windus, London, 1958, chapters 3 and 4.

5 Catholic Action is not easily defined. For Pope Pius X1, according to historian Patrick O'Farrell, it 'amounted to the organisational involvement of the laity in the apostolic work of the church, under the guidance of the bishops, in those areas of life with which the church had lost contact', especially the working class. But 'except for Archbishop Mannix, the Australian hierarchy of the 1930s showed little awareness of the social emphasis given by the Pope. The Archbishop of Sydney, Dr Kelly, in a 1934 pastoral letter, defined Catholic Action to mean "Catholics living exemplary lives, joining together in hearing the word of God and keeping it".' Patrick O'Farrell, *The Catholic Church and Community in Australia*, Nelson, West Melbourne, 1977, p. 384.

6 Colin R. Jory, *The Campion Society and Catholic Social Militancy in Australia, 1929–1939.* With a Foreword by Manning Clark. Harpham, Kogarah, New South Wales, 1986.

7 Vincent Buckley, *Cutting Green Hay*, Penguin Books, Ringwood, 1983, p. 142.

4 New Haven Winter

1 Peter Rose to Brenda Niall, 8 August 2006.

2 Edith Wharton, *A Backward Glance*, New York, Appleton Century, 1934, p. 73.

3 Millicent Bell, *Edith Wharton and Henry James*, Braziller, New York, 1965, p. 315.

4 Ibid, p. 6.

5 Matching the Matriarchs: Ethel Turner and Mary Grant Bruce

1 Ivan Southall, *A Journey of Discovery*, Harmondsworth, Middlesex, 1975, pp. 68–9.

2 HV Evatt to Ethel Turner, 14 December 1939, Turner Papers, Mitchell Library, State Library of New South Wales, MS 667/12/197.

3 Philippa Poole, (comp.) *The Diaries of Ethel Turner*, Ure Smith, Sydney, 1979, June–August 1892, *passim.*

4 Henry Lawson to Miles Franklin, September 1902. Quoted by AW Barker (ed.), in *Dear Robertson: Letters to an Australian Publisher*, Angus and Robertson, Sydney, 1982, p. 34.

6 Walking upon Ashes: In the Footsteps of Martin Boyd

1 Samuel Johnson, 'Addison', *Lives of the English Poets*, George Birkbeck Hill (ed.), Oxford, 1905, vol 2, p. 116.

2 Geoffrey Dutton, *Out in the Open: an Autobiography*, University of Queensland Press, Brisbane, 1994, p. 412.

3 Ibid.
4 Sam Wood spoke of 'Marge' Michell, and was not sure if her name was Marjorie or Margaret. He remembered her as a tall, elegant woman.
5 Barbara Gill to Sam Wood, n.d [1972].
6 Leon Edel, Preface, *Henry James: a Life*, Collins, London, 1985.
7 Michael Holroyd, *Basil Street Blues: a Family Story*, Little, Brown, London, 1999, p. 144.
8 Hermione Lee, *Body Parts: Essays in Life-writing*, Chatto, London, 2005, p. 216.
9 David Boyd, 'An Open House', *Bulletin* (Sydney), 23–30 December 1980.

7 Searching for the Subject: Georgiana McCrae

1 James Walter, 'Biography, Psychobiography and Cultural Space', in Ian Donaldson, Peter Read and James Walter, (eds), *Shaping Lives: Reflections on Biography*, Australian National University, Humanities Research Centre, Canberra, 1992, p. 264.
2 Georgiana McCrae to Edie Anderson, 7 June 1887. McCrae Family Papers, State Library of Victoria.
3 R.W. Chapman, (ed.), *Boswell's Life of Johnson*, OUP, 1952 p. 625.

8 Group Portrait: The Boyds

1 Leon Edel, *Bloomsbury: a House of Lions*, Hogarth Press, London, 1979, p. 12.
2 Robin Boyd, 'Under Tension', *Architectural Review* (London), vol. 134, no. 181, November 1963, p. 334.
3 id., *The Australian Ugliness*, F.W. Cheshire, Melbourne, p. 251.

9 Face to Face: Judy Cassab

1 Richard Holmes, *Sidetracks*, HarperCollins, London, 2000, p. 4.
2 Lou Klepac, *Judy Cassab: Portraits of Artists and Friends*, Beagle Press, Sydney, 1998, p. 16.

10 Time Capsule: Finding Father Hackett

1 William Hackett to Florence Hackett, n.d., [March 1952], Hackett Papers, Jesuit Archives, Hawthorn, Victoria.
2 William Hackett to Mary (Mollie) Childers, 26 November 1922, Childers Papers, Trinity College Library, Dublin, MS7487-51-478.
3 Lloyd George's contentious *Act for the Restoration of Order in Ireland*, 1920, prohibited the possession of documents likely to incite unlawful behaviour.

Index

Where two or more family members share the same name, birth and/or death dates have been given to avoid confusion.